Write your eBook or Other Short Book—Fast!

Bonus Reports

Promoting Books @ The Speed of Thought

How to Get Testimonials from the Rich and Famous

The Top Ten Secrets of Successful Authors

Top Ten eBook Mistakes and How to Correct Them

Print on Demand (POD) Publishers – the Good, the Bad, and the Ugly

Write your eBook or Other Short Book—Fast!

Judy Cullins

Skills Unlimited Publishing
bookcoaching.com

In association with

Your Own World Books
yowbooks.com

Other Books by Judy Cullins

Ten Non-techie Ways to Market Your Book Online

Quadruple Online Sales in Four Months with Free Articles

Power Writing for Web Sites That Sell

The Fast and Cheap Way to Explode Targeted Web Traffic

Mindmapping—Another Way to Outline your Book and Chapters

Seven Sure-Fire Ways to Publicize your Business

How to Submit Your Articles to Top Web Sites: Step-by-Step

How to Write and Sell Your Book Fast Kit (Print 5-Book Kit)

How to Get Testimonials From the Rich and Famous

Market Your Books Through an eNewsletter

Seven Sure-Fire Ways to Sell a Lot of Books (Offline To Do's)

Your Book's Marketing Plan—Launch, First Year and Beyond

Use Powerwords to Spice Up Every Page of Your Book or Web Site

Sell Your Book to Libraries

Radio and TV Publicity – Become a Household Name

Write a Power Press Release to Get a Feature Story

The Big Three Marketing Machine

How to Write a Query and One-Page Book Proposal

Copyright

Copyright 2005 by Judy Cullins
All rights Reserved
DOI: 10.1572/judy.cullins

First Yowbooks Edition 2005
DOI: 10.1572/jcl.writeyourebook

Paperback
ISBN: 978-1-59772-020-5
DOI: 10.1572/9781597720205

Adobe eBook
ISBN: 978-1-59772-021-2
DOI: 10.1572/9781597720212

Microsoft eBook
ISBN: 978-1-59772-022-9
DOI: 10.1572/9781597720229

Mobipocket eBook
ISBN: 978-1-59772-023-6
DOI: 10.1572/9781597720236

Palm eBook
ISBN: 978-1-59772-024-3
DOI: 10.1572/9781597720243

SKILLS UNLIMITED PUBLISHING
bookcoaching.com

In association with

YOUR OWN WORLD BOOKS
an imprint of Your Own World, Inc.
Carson City, NV USA
DOI: 10.1572/yowbooks
SAN: 256-1646
yowbooks.com

What people are saying about this book...

"This is not a book on how to write. It is a book on how to get it written. It is full of the shortcuts, experiences and tips only an insider could know. Whether you are working on an eBook or a pBook, you will find Judy Cullins' wisdom invaluable."

—Dan Poynter,
The Self Publishing Manual, Writing Non-Fiction.

"Whoever said 'Fifty percent of writing is getting the first word on a blank piece of paper' should have had Judy Cullins' book! It's inspiring and practical, an unbeatable combination. *Write Your eBook or Other Short Book—Fast!* offers checklists, tips, tricks and the encouragement you need to get your book out of your head and onto the shelves. If you've ever thought of writing a book or even written one but want to improve the process, get this book."

—Mary Westheimer,
CEO, BookZone.com

"Save yourself from headaches, disappointments, and money down the drain. Read *Write Your eBook or Other Short Book—Fast!* before you write another word. Judy puts you on the fastest track to publishing success."

—Marcia Reynolds, M.A., M.Ed.,
Past president of the International Coach Federation,
How to Outsmart Your Brain and Capture the Rapture

"Want to make money while you sleep? E-books are in and anyone can write them—particularly if you sit at the feet of someone who has gone before you. Get this book and get the secrets. Then write one of your own."

—Joe Vitale,
Hypnotic Writing

Table of Contents

Introduction

Inside a story brews, information you must share! Unique, needed information you know will benefit lives—hundreds and thousands of lives.

Where are you now with your book? Discouraged you don't know how? It will take too long? Be too much work? Cost too much money? Do you worry it won't be good enough to sell? Whether you are an emerging or already published author, *Write Your EBook or Other Short Book—Fast!* shows you each step of the way to market while you write, publish quickly, and not make the mistakes even seasoned authors make—all to make you a successful author!

We authors write the books we need; thus, after my twenty years of writing, publishing and selling books, this book has evolved to give you an easy-to-use formula to write a quality book fast.

Each chapter gives short, no-nonsense "how-to" answers to your questions, "author's tips," and Internet resources to help you market.

With your passion, intention, attention, and patience, you will finish your treasured book years before you would taking the agent/publisher route. You'll get respect for being an expert, your business will flourish, you'll make lifetime income, and you'll love the adventure. So, turn the page and begin now!

Judy Cullins
La Mesa, CA

Why Write an eBook or Other Short Book?

Are you a speaker, seminar leader, consultant, coach, writer, author, or small business owner? The book you write sharing your unique, useful message will expand your life at least ten-fold. Each of you has your own reason to write. You also have advantages. Here are eighteen reasons and advantages to spur you on to write your book! Put check marks next to the ones that are important to you.

1. Recognition—people value your message.
2. Fame—authors are in the top 10% of professions.
3. Stimulating life—full of adventure and opportunities.
4. Expression of your personal mission to help others.
5. Standing out from the crowd.
6. Attracting much more business profits.
7. Credibility—more than any other product.
8. An ongoing, consistent profit center.
9. Raises your perceived value as a businessperson.
10. Brings you a form of immortality.
11. Authors can live anywhere.
12. Expands your visibility, especially on the Internet.
13. Brands your business—you will always be in business.
14. A cost effective way to multiply sales.
15. Ongoing passive/active income.
16. Entry to Radio and TV shows, corporations, and guest spots on tele-classes.

17. Your book is your best business card.

18. People need and want your unique, useful, message.

Author's Tip: A book brings you more credibility than any other product: tapes, CD-ROM's, videos, or games.

The one question most book clients ask is "But will my book be good enough to interest my audience?"

Of course you don't want to waste your time writing a bad book. One important ingredient in your book is your passion. So, if you love your topic or you're anxious to learn more about it—that's passion enough! An author starts with passion and then adds other ingredients to make their books captivate their readers. Take the test below to discover whether your book will be significant enough.

Test Your Book's Significance

1. Is it filled with action? Is it Exciting?

2. Is it fun to read? Does it have humor?

3. Does it teach the reader something interesting? New?

4. Does it present useful/original/unique information?

5. Does it have the potential to positively affect the reader's life?

6. Is its message said in a unique way?

7. Does it answer an age-old question like the meaning of life?

8. Does it create a deeper understanding of human nature?

9. Does it give skills and information to help individuals?

10. Will the book's particular audience want or need its information?

Of the ten significances it takes only...

• One for a newspaper or magazine article

• Two for a book

• Three for a top seller

• Five for a Pulitzer prize

- Six for a literary classic

- So, be encouraged and start writing!

How Can You Write a Book That Sells?

Your book has enough significance. You have something valuable to share with the world. You have a personal story that others can learn from. You have a business and know a book will make you more credible. You are ready to take the next step to join the top 10% of professions: authorship.

If you aren't sure what topic you would like to write on, check out the tips below. Start with a topic that sells well.

Seven Ways to Select a Topic That Sells

1. Write what you are passionate about. Write about a topic that will still interest you in two years. Your book is an extension of you, your talks, and your profession. If you don't love your topic, you won't be successful. One common mistake authors make is to put attention on writing another book before there first one has been promoted.

2. Write down five topics that stir your passion. Ask your inner author which one should you pay attention to first. After choosing, gather and organize everything you already know and want to know about that topic. If you need more knowledge on a topic, research it. Read other authors' books in your field, check out related Web sites, and subscribe to newsletters. You become the expert as you write.

3. Write a book your audience needs or wants. People want their problems solved. Among fourteen other books, three on memory and a speed-reading manual I wrote 15 years ago have sold over 55,000 copies, and still sell today. Business books sell well. People need writing, reading, speaking, computing, communication, math, sales, marketing and Internet skills. Nonfiction self-help or how to titles sell best. When your nonfiction books sells well, you can finance your novel.

4. Research your target market. Who is your preferred audience? Who will read and buy your book? Who will pay the $15-$35 price tag? How many possible buyers are there? How does your book stack up to your competition? What is your unique selling proposition? What benefits does your book bring its readers? How many in your audience? According to Dan Poynter, author of *Writing Nonfiction*, an audience of 200,000 to 700,000 is best. The targeted book *Chicken*

Soup for the Teenage Soul sold three million copies more in one year than the original *Chicken Soup* sold in three years.

5. Compare your book with other reputable, good sellers in your field. What way is your book like theirs? What makes your book unique from others? How is your book better? If your book is the only one of its kind, it could be more difficult to sell because mainstream buyers don't know about it. Check out what category your book fits in by visiting your local bookstore. Ask the bookseller to help you. Turn to the back covers–look at the upper left side to see the two or three categories usually listed there. Which ones does your book fit under? Let your book develop a new angle on the problem to be solved. A book on breast-feeding sold far more copies when the author aimed it at working mothers.

6. Survey your market. While some of us get our title instantly and know that it is the right one, many of us need help. Brainstorm with, and ask for feedback from, friends and associates. Let them vote on the best of ten titles and subtitles, chapter titles, back cover information. While some get their title instantly and know it's the right one, many of us need help. Knowing that titles are the top "Essential Hot Selling Point" makes time spent on it worth it. When you use the synergy of more brainpower, you receive so many more ideas. Don't be attached to your choices. Feedback helps build a better book.

7. Create a winning vision for your book. Know that your book will be published. Specifically name the outcomes you will see, hear and feel. Place this winning vision in color on a card. Put it near your workstation. (Using today's date including the year) Now that my book (title and subtitle) is finished and is a huge seller. For example:

I **see** (smiling people at my talks buying it)

I **hear** (applause from multiple audiences affirming it)

I **feel** (exhilarated, confident and pleased that it's such a hit)

What Makes One Book Outsell Another?

What's the point of writing a book if it doesn't sell well? Here, you can discover ways to make your book more marketable.

1. Write a book that people need and want. People want how-to books, they want skills. Notice the demand today for eBooks. It's best to see

the need and fill it rather than have an idea and then look for an audience.

2. Write and market non-fiction books first. They account for about seventy-five percent of total book sales. You can use your profits to finance a fiction project.

3. Write short books in any format, such as eBooks, booklets, guides or special reports.

    They are faster, easier, and cheaper to write than full-length books of 150-300 pages. They can be as short as five pages (special reports), to eBooks that can be 10-100 pages. A common mistake of emerging authors is that they write books that are too long. Today's audience wants fast, easy-to-read information. Ask yourself if you would rather read a long how-to book or a short one. Divide and conquer. Put most closely-related chapters into one book; then, put other related chapters into another one. Most book coaching clients write books of ninety pages or less in length.

4. Angle your book toward women. They buy far more books than men do, accounting for about seventy-five percent of book purchases. If your message benefits women, you'll do well in sales. The *Chicken Soup for Women* series sold 20 million copies out of 68 million for the total series sold.

5. Choose your title with care. Image is almost everything. Your front cover and title have from 5-10 seconds to impress your potential buyer. Be clear, use metaphor and make sure your visuals connect to your title. Elicit an emotion through your title words (preferably 5-7 words). What solutions and results does your book promise? Include these in your title if possible.

6. Expand your book into a series. Think of the huge success of the *Chicken Soup* Series. They have one "brand" everyone recognizes.

7. Create spin-off products that relate to your book. Some people prefer to learn by listening to a cassette, downloading a file or purchasing a CD-ROM. I recently bought a serial eBook and loved getting two chapters a week—so easy to digest. On the Internet, you can make your book an e-course, and charge much more money than for an eBook. These formats can actually help you sell more books. Other spin-offs include coaching, consulting, speaking, seminars, teaching teleclasses, writing or making videos.

8. Impress your potential buyer within fifteen seconds with your back cover copy. At the top put your headline, not the title. It must hook

your readers, stir up their emotions, and hit their desires. What benefits does your book offer? How to get more money, heart-centered relationships, more fame, or more health? Include from 3-5 bullets of what your book promises its readers and those important testimonials.

9. Create your written book-marketing plan as you write your book. This plan covers your first year's launch period and lifetime plan. The biggest mistake new authors make is that they quit marketing after the initial six months. Word-of-mouth takes a while. Be patient and market your book for up to three years. Another mistake is that inexperienced authors wait until publication before they think of marketing, losing a great deal of sales. Your plan could include a list of your book's essential hot-selling points, how much income you want to make per month, your 30-second tell-and-sell, book reviews, news releases, articles to market your book, the book signings, talks, electronic newsletters, and a book Web site. Without a written plan, an author creates vague results.

10. Put as much time into marketing as you did the writing of your book. Remember that writing a book costs you time and money. Marketing and promotion make you money. Your goal is to have people read and learn from your unique message. Why plant a garden if you don't harvest it? After I opened up to the Internet by getting high school computer/techie mentors, sales from my book went from $75 in one month to over $3000 in eight months. And, after four years, this income keeps growing. All because of marketing in an easier and more inexpensive way than the traditional one. Put some effort into learning new ways to market. Books are the number one product sold on the Internet, and there's little competition using Internet promotion methods. .

11. Include Web marketing to sell more books. While you can sell your books on other people's' Web sites, such as Amazon.com or Booklocker.com, you eventually will want your own. An author without a Web site is like a person without a name. Your site can contain plenty of free content, such as articles related to your book's topic. Include testimonials, archived ezines and excerpts from your book. If you want to sell from your site, be sure to include a sales letter for each product or service. Change your content often to attract more returning visitors. These are your potential buyers.

Another big question you may have is "Will my book sell enough copies to satisfy my financial requirements?"

You are already busy. You wonder if you will have the time, know-how, and money to finish the project, and will it be worth your efforts?

One solution is to start small with an article, a special report or eBook. When you have a group of related topics, you can bundle them to make a longer eBook. These sell well, especially on the Internet. No one wants to have a storage area full of unsold books, so in today's publishing game, you should print only the copies you can sell in six months. One of my clients sold 91 copies of her humor book before her books were even printed! The new Print on Demand technology slashes publishing costs. (See Chapter Four and special bonus report.)

Now that you know your book has significance, will stand out from the crowd, and sell well, read on in Chapter Two to write your chapters in half the time with fewer edits to get your chapters together fast.

Write Your Chapters in Half the Time With Fewer Edits

Do you have a problem creating a focus in your non-fiction chapters? Does your writing slip around, leaving a muddy path to the gold–your unique, useful message? Do your fiction chapters need to be fuller? Do they answer all of your reader questions about the who, what, when, where, how and why?

Format each non-fiction chapter in your book. Your consistency, your organized, focused copy will compel your reader to want to read every chapter because they are easy to understand.

You'll write much faster because you pose three to eight questions your audience wants answered, and as you answer them, the questions become the headlines throughout your chapter. Without engaging headlines throughout your chapter, your audience may get lost and lose motivation to keep reading.

Remember what your audience wants.

For your non-fiction or self-help book, they have a number one question they want solved. For instance, in this book, it's how to write a book fast. Next, they want each chapter to have one focus and a topic that supports the title or thesis statement. In this book, the chapter on how to format your chapter fast asks the question how and answers it. Your other chapter titles also support the thesis such as how the essential "hot selling points" help pre-market your book in chapter 3 of this book.

The number one mistake most new writers make is to start writing a chapter before they are sure of the main idea that will be its center. In a short book called *Beat Procrastination*, each chapter gave a particular way to overcome it. One chapter talked about why we procrastinate. To make it clear and easy to read, the author laid out an introduction with a hook, then listed and dis-

cussed fear of success, fear of failure, incomplete information, and fear of dis-
cipline. She did it through the art of asking and answering questions. She
ended it with three action steps to take.

Before you write any chapters except Chapter One (it's sometimes an introduction), make sure you have a focus and three to eight questions ready to
answer.

> **Author's Tip:** You don't have to write chapter one first. Choose a chapter
> that is easy for you to relate to, one you already have a lot of information
> on. See the format workbook below. This idea defies the myth that you
> need to research your book. It's all inside you right now.

The chapter that sells is the one that is easy-to-read.

Steps to Formatting Each Non-Fiction Chapter

I also don't think you should center the One. It would look better at far left as
I had it originally.

One: Your Chapter's Opening-Introduction

Like your book introduction, you need to open each chapter with a hook to
grab your reader by the collar, to engage her, and relate to her challenge or
problem. In just a sentence or two, you can open in these ways: several
thought-provoking questions or shocking facts that relate to your reader's
challenge. After the hook, let the readers know your thesis—that may include
benefits of reading this chapter.

Remember the payoffs of a great chapter format: you will write faster, with
fewer edits, be more organized, be more compelling, and your writing will be
easy to read.

In personal growth books, many authors like to open with a famous quote that
reflects the particular chapter's main idea.

The chapter opening should be fairly short—maybe one or two paragraphs.

Author's Tip: A big mistake emerging authors make is to tell their story with an "I" point of view. Your readers don't care about you, they read on because you can help them solve their challenge. If you do include information about yourself, introduce it so you include your audience. For instance. Like me, perhaps you too had this challenge.

Two: Your Chapter's Middle—The Answers to your Readers' Questions—The How-to's

Each chapter's middle, where you share your stories or how-to's needs two things: a compelling or at least clear heading and a short introduction with a hook so your reader will want to keep reading.

Personal or business coaches or consultants can use a client's story to illustrate a point. Then, as the savvy professional, the consultant gives the solutions that evolved from the client's questions or their own wisdom.

Another kind of story is a success story that gives the readers the savvy information they look for.

Other examples include: making a question that applies to this chapter into a headline, then answering it with a number of tips, how to's, check lists, resources, sidebars or quotes. To see examples, check out some best-selling books in your subject.

Sprinkled throughout your chapter, you may place author tips indented ten spaces to fit just the middle part of the page. Or, put them into boxes. People love tips that are short and easy. They love to take away wisdom. You may choose to do the same for related quotes, as Julia Cameron did in *Artists Way*. Don't add random quotes just because you like them. Make sure they support each chapter's focus.

Three: Your Non-Fiction's Chapter's End

Your reader expects a finish at each chapter's end. They want a summary, a chapter review or action steps to take away. Give them fieldwork, too. They want to know why they should read the next chapter.

To end your chapter with a bang, you may want to leave your reader with questions to ponder, and for the last paragraph, write a few lines that include benefits to lead them into the next chapter.

Author's Tip on Branding: Branding your book sets it apart from all the others. Notice famous self-help authors using their title's brand throughout their book. You can brand your book title and each chapter title within it, too. You can also brand parts, such as sidebars and tips that you put into each chapter.

For a book called *Passion at Any Age,* I rewrote each chapter title to mention a form of the word, "passion." In the annotated Chapter One "Attracting Passion" title, benefits included were: "Expand fulfillment, overcome resistance, communicate clearly and come from the heart." Within each chapter, like me, you can brand your tips or other side matter. "Passion Hot Line Tips" support the book's title.

You can brand your business like one business client of mine did. He changed his book title many times, but finally he used *The Smiling Owner-How to Build a Great Small Business.* He added a visual that every business owner can connect to. He worked the "Smiling Owner" metaphor into his how to's and tips throughout his chapters.

Format each chapter in your book. Your consistency, your organized, focused copy will compel your reader to want to read every chapter, because they are easy to understand.

Author's Tip: All chapters except Chapter One should be approximately the same length. (See the coming examples of questions you can ask for non-fiction, self-help and fiction to figure out how long your chapters will be).

Chapter Format Workbook

Here is a template guide to fill in with all the format parts of one chapter. Use this model and input your own information under the various headings. Remember, if this doesn't fit, you can "color outside these lines" with my full encouragement.

This consistent format helps your readers get a hold of your points and take away understanding and appreciation for your clarity and focus.

But first, you need to make a list of topics, questions that your audience wants answered. After your long list for the whole book, divide these into categories that you can put into chapters, about five to seven questions for one chapter.

Author's Note: Be sure to keep a file in your book folder labeled "whole book questions," or "chapter one questions."

Preparation for Each Chapter

- Make a list of your audience's challenges this chapter will solve.

- Make a list of this chapter's benefits (the outcomes they can see and feel).

To Write Each Non-Fiction Chapter with Focus and Power

Chapter Title—Use a working title or topic if you don't know. Write it here.

Chapter Thesis—Write in one sentence the # one focus of the chapter.

Chapter Introduction—Hook in opening or introduction—Include questions where audience is now. Take them from your list of audience challenges or problems.

- Hook your reader in the opening lines of your introduction—Can be a pertinent quote, or 1, 2 or 3 questions about where your audience is now before they read this chapter. Stressed? Tired? Unfocused in your work? Your opener must hook the reader to keep reading. Speak to their issues, not your story.

- End the opener with a thesis statement. "In this chapter you will be aware of...learn...discover...if that works for you. Think of the thesis as the number one question this chapter will answer. Here is a good spot to include the chapter benefits. Make sure all the rest of the chapter supports this thesis.

So go ahead, name your chapter and write one chapter's hook here:

Now, write this chapter's thesis:

Create the chapter's middle.

This part of your chapter is the meat; the stories and tips you offer your reader to help solve their challenge or know more about a topic.

Next, create a list of questions that support the thesis or main idea. These questions will become the headings for this part of your chapter. They help your reader stay on track and get answers .These questions are the skeleton, the bare bones, to which you will add the flesh of anecdotes, stories, tips, how-to's, practices, or sidebars. A question can turn into a statement in the chapter title, it can name the headings and subheadings, and the how to exercises.

Author's Note: A chapter without headings loses your reader, because they don't know where they are going.

Answers to your posed questions are like benefits and are what make your reader satisfied they got their money's worth in your chapter. You may pose a question, then answer it with stories, tips, how-to's, inspiration in other forms. The features of your chapter include its pictures, author's note and sidebars with pertinent information

Author's Tip: It's a good idea to include a hook after each heading too. Again, you ask a few questions where the reader is now on this topic. This serves as an introduction and engages your reader to want to read the rest. Much better than just telling them what to do. Engage your reader continuously throughout your chapters.

List your chapter questions here. Write as much of your middle as you can here. If you have holes in your information, find other resources to help you. But always, make this information your own.

The Chapter End—action steps, last paragraph inviting them into next chapter

If you write non-fiction, your chapter needs a summary, action steps, ideas to ponder and finishing statement– a final one or two sentence paragraph to lead your reader from this chapter to the next. You may want to include the next chapter's thesis and a few questions it will answer.

Author's Note: To finish writing your chapters fast put a few words and phrases down, so you can feel you can write. Even if they are not the right words, they give you something to build on. It's easier to hook new ideas onto thoughts already expressed. So, copy and paste this blueprint into your book's folder for each chapter. You'll be amazed at how much faster you will write—and it will be so much easier with the Q and A format.

Sample Chapter Format Review

Book Title: Quadruple your Sales in Four Months with Articles

Chapter Title: The Top Ten Reasons to Write Articles to Market your Book

Chapter Thesis: Market your Book Through Free Articles.

Opening-Hook-Thesis: Has traditional marketing let you down? Would you like to make many more monthly book sales? In this chapter learn why writing short how-to tips and articles are the #1 Way to Promote your Books and Services.

Middle: Headlines with each benefit discussed and success story to illustrate how one person's articles brought her new product and service sales.

End: Give resistances for doing something new such as Internet marketing. Then follow with action steps and ideas to move the beginner or non-techie into readiness to expand her book through the net.

> **Author's Note:** The benefits of asking and answering questions ahead of time before you write are: you have a road map to follow to make your chapters more organized, compelling and easy to read. One added bonus-you write and finish so much faster.

> **Author's Note:** For Your Longer Book—Answer more questions in each chapter for your reader. In a longer book of 145 pages or so, with 10 chapters, its chapter format will be more detailed. If you want around 12 pages per chapter, you will want to pose and answer 12 questions. If you want a shorter chapter just know that the number of answered questions will just about equal the number of 8 ½ by 11 pages. When you translate your book to 6 by 9 or 5 by 8 your book's pages will be longer.

Sample Questions That Became Chapter Titles from How to Write Your eBook or Other Book—Fast!

1. Why should I write a book? The advantages of writing a Book

2. How can I write a saleable book? What does it take to write a great-selling book?

3. How can I write my book in less time with fewer edits?

Where Do You Get Your Questions for Your Self-Help Book?

Your non fiction books will solve problems and challenges for your readers. You may start with questions your audience has about particular problems or challenges.

You have already heard these when you are out and about because many of the people you meet are your preferred audience. When you finish your audience profile (see Chapter on "Essential-Hot-Selling-Points.") you will have plenty of audience questions and concerns you can solve in your chapters.

In Spencer Johnson's short book, ***The One-Minute Sales Person***, he chose to answer seven general questions that became his seven chapters titles.

In each of his chapters, he chose other particular questions to answer.

In chapter one, he answered the question, "What is the book's purpose?" Many authors answer this question in their introduction.

In chapter two, the author answered several questions about how to act "before the sale." His how-to's included: "First, I see others getting what they want, then I see me getting what I want." (Visualize the customer happy) Second, "I learn the difference between features and benefits of what I sell." Third, "I see the benefits of what I sell actually helping others get the feelings they want."

Spencer's chapter format is first, a summary, then a delightful story interwoven.

The rest of the chapter titles are: 3. During the Sale; 4. After the Sale; 5. My One-Minute Goals; 6. My One-Minute Praisings; and 7. My One-Minute Reprimands. These chapter titles make up the book's table of contents.

Notice in his book of 100 pages, the author needed to answer only seven major questions. In each chapter, he answered three to seven questions that added content to his bare bones outline.

> **Author's Tip:** Chapter titles, like book titles, should be clear, concise and compelling. If your titles are clever, but not clear, you must have a subtitle. Your chapter titles will later become your Table of Contents, another "Essential-Hot-Selling Point."

If You are Writing Fiction...

Both nonfiction and fiction use stories. Personal experiences, anecdotes, dialogue or inner dialogue, and stories are great ways to start any chapter. You can intersperse throughout your non-fiction chapters. The discussion below is for your fiction book.

In fiction, you also want to answer your readers' questions. First, the Number One Ultimate Reader's Question. You may not answer this one until the end of your book, but it's best to know it before you write the book. It could be, "did the main character overcome his challenge?" You know where your story is going by knowing this answer before you write a single chapter. Now you can write the rest of your story with confidence and include the right details to make your reader satisfied.

How to Open your First Fiction Chapter

A beginning chapter shows the initiating incident that leads to the darkest moment or character's challenges. Your main character's desires are thwarted now and along the way—making necessary conflict. Share your main character's desires, goals, and dreams in the beginning. Show the emotional tug of war. Reveal your character's problems and fears. What is she afraid of losing? What worries him? Make this chapter shine by showing your main character's obstacles. Include conflict (see below) to give your story plenty of action.

> **Author's Tip:** The biggest mistake emerging and seasoned authors make is to not have enough action in their story. Your audience today wants action. You must grab your reader by the collar, draw them into your character's world, and provoke their continued interest through conflict. Avoid too much description or narrative unless it moves your story forward.

Which Fiction Chapter Opening is Best for You?

1. Launch your story with an external conflict, a character trait or flaw, or a physical problem. Audiences love character driven stories and they love a character with challenges and problems.

2. Show your character's ordinary world so your reader can bond with her. Catch a glimpse of your character's dream or essence. A rude awakening can be the inciting event. Keep this to one page or so.

3. Start with the most exciting part of your story. Here, you begin with action, actually in the middle of things or in the thick of conflict. Good storytellers admire this classic beginning. This opening really hooks the reader. It offers a preview of the most intense conflict. One memoir started with the brutal divorce; the other chapters told of how the heroine grew into a successful life. After chapter one, you go back in time to show how the mess got started. Don't choose this if the conflict should surprise the reader in the middle of the story.

4. Begin with the Now and Go Back to Then

    Here, you begin the action in the present day such as attending a wedding, funeral, or reunion. The past hurtles toward you like a pie in the face. You may include the first time you met this person who affected you so deeply. This inciting incident starts your story, and ends up with the reunion, showing what happened in-between.

5. Give a portrait of your character or your setting.

    For some writers this is a strong way to open a story. Your description precipitates the conflict. You can also start with an engaging description of the setting where the conflict occurs. *Angela's Ashes* starts this way.

6. Open your story with early memories and tell it chronologically.

    Here you arrange your story with earliest memories and incidents to continue with the most interesting events. You may arrange by decades or personal milestones. This style can be dull unless the writer is sharp. Yet, its advantage is that it's simple and clear.

7. Name alternate chapters with your two main characters. This is the winning style of *Cold Mountain*.

Create your Five-Minute Lead for One Chapter at a Time

Three Steps

1. Start your lead in every chapter with the most interesting or dramatic part of your story. Your lead must create more questions than your story answers. It does this by jumping right into the scene and briefly describing the "what" or "who" of the action without bothering to answer the "how" or "why."

2. Give your readers a reason to want to read your opening chapter pages, and then finish the chapter. Powerwords create a reader buzz. When they finish chapter after chapter, they will really recommend your book to their friends and associates.

    Like an artist, a writer paints with words and metaphors. They exude powerful emotions and perceptions through these riveting phrases and words. "Powerwords" attract your readers' attention and compel them to read on.

    Think about the word "rape," belying a tragedy, a power struggle, dark and dangerous. Any word promoting emotion draws in your readers' hearts.

"Powerwords" can make a dull chapter zing! They produce strong reactions, positive, and negative. Some "Powerwords" make you smile, others, cringe. Some stimulate the senses while others exude a fragrant aroma or flavorful taste.

"Powerwords" refer to nouns and verbs. They show a picture, reveal an emotion and help create dazzling metaphors. When you use powerful nouns and verbs, you won't need to use adjectives and adverbs that merely tell.

3. Jot down some ideas, words, and phrases about your chapter. Instead of ordinary sentence starters, choose five or so of the most powerful words. List them now. Then make the first word or form of the word the first of several sentences. Power words are words that emit emotion, are visual and dramatic.

    1. _____   2. _____

    3. _____   4. _____

    5. _____   6. _____

Look at your list of power words you jotted down. Which three words attract you the most? Of these, which are the two least interesting? Take the most powerful and make the first word of your opening lead that one or a form of it. For instance, "rape," rapist, raping or "slam," slamming, slammed, slam-dunk. One great lead is to open with dialogue. "Rape! Rape!" she yelled in the Vons parking lot.

Usual "ho-hum" chapter openers start with words like "the," "a," "it," or a personal pronoun like "he." Your opener must hook and entertain your reader so he will finish your chapter and want more. This technique works for non-fiction as well as fiction. Use the other "powerwords" you listed in the rest of the opening lead, consisting of three or four paragraphs.

Now, on a separate piece of paper or straight onto your computer, write your opening lead. Answer the questions that, what's going on, what conflict takes place, what action goes on?

What did you learn from this exercise?

-   To have a starting plan

-   To sparkle writing with spectacular words

-   To be more concise

Having a Lead and having an Ultimate Reader Question is what keeps the story beginning and the story ending completely separate from the story middle. It's the most effective way in the world to write a real three-part story with a clearly defined beginning, middle, and end.

Once you have your opening lead done, you need to make the rest of your chapter full and rich Use the lists of possible questions to answer below.

Make Each Chapter Shine with Your Easy Fiction Blue Print

For a real page-turner, you need to answer the most important questions your readers have within the first 30 pages. What's at stake? Why should I care?

You can start writing any chapter to apply this "Question and Answer" fiction-writing approach. Each chapter practically writes itself. Your benefits? You spend less time– one-half the edits; you write more focused, rich language chapters; and you answer the questions your hungry readers want to know.

The following are questions for fiction writers to answer in writing. Answer only the ones that apply to your book. Just write one or two questions per category and answer in long hand or put notes on your computer. Keep these notes by your computer when you are ready to write the first draft. Not only will you write faster, but your writing will flow, be more natural, and be more organized.

Six Categories of Questions to Choose From for Each Chapter

To flush out your chapters, to make them full of conflict and action, the following categories will help. Choose a few from each category; write them down. Answer them on the paper or on your computer. Keep them by your document and refer to them when you need to. After you once write the questions and answers, you won't need to refer to your paper probably. The best benefits? Your writing is easy, flows, and is totally natural.

Samples of the Six Categories

Who: Who is the viewpoint character? The hero? Let your readers know your character.

What: What will happen in the first scene? (Start your story with the most exciting part—the hook) What does the viewpoint character want? What is the conflict? (Without conflict, you don't have action, and without action, your readers will yawn. What emotion do you want your reader to feel?

Where: Where does it take place?

When: When does it take place? The year?

How: How does the character triumph? Fail? Struggle?

Why: Why does the character triumph? Fail? Struggle?

Or, just choose one-three from these Question Categories.

Who

1. Who is the most likeable person in this chapter?

2. Who is the most unlikable person in this chapter?

3. Who is the hero or villain of this chapter?

4. Who inspired the character(s) to do what they're doing in this chapter?

5. Who was the direct or indirect cause of the biggest problems encountered in this chapter?

6. Who gave the important advice to your character concerning the events that take place in this chapter?

7. Who taught your character to be able to do what they are doing?

8. Who is the most beautiful or ugliest person in this chapter?

9. Who are some of the other characters who will be ultimately affected by what happens in this chapter?

Note: Which two or three questions do you want to answer to later include when you write each chapter on your computer? Have them ready when you schedule 2 hours to input a chapter.

What

1. What is the worst or best thing that happens in this chapter?

2. What was the attraction that caused the character to get involved with this incident?

3. What is the most touching or heart-warming thing that happens in this chapter?

4. What important lesson do you want your audience to learn in this chapter?

5. What was your character's most regrettable action in this chapter?

6. What is the most colorful thing to see or the most colorful place your character visits in this chapter?

7. What was the one single smell that was most prevalent in this chapter setting?

8. What was the most interesting sound that your character heard or uttered in this chapter?

9. What did the main character learn "after the fact" that they wish they would have known before the experience told about in this chapter?

Note: Which 2 or 3 questions do you want to answer to later include when you write each chapter on your computer? Have them ready when you schedule 2 hours to input a chapter. Maybe you won't use any in this category.

When

1. When was your character's luckiest moment in this chapter?

2. When was your character's unluckiest moment in this chapter?

3. When did this incident begin...what year or what time?

4. When was the problem first noticed?

5. When was a solution to the problem first thought of?

6. When did the trouble begin to get out of hand?

7. When were the seeds first planted that led to this happening?

8. When does the character finally get on the right track?

9. When does this particular incident come to an end?

Note: Which two or three questions do you want to answer to later include when you write each chapter on your computer? Have them ready when you schedule 2 hours to input a chapter. Maybe you won't use any in this category.

Where

1. Where is the most interesting looking place in this part of the story, what does it look like?

2. Where is the character trying to get to?

3. Where does the character wind up at the end of this chapter?

4. Where does your character make a big mistake in this part of their recorded experience?

5. Where is the most beautiful setting in your chapter?

6. Where does the chapter start?

7. Where did the character come from to get to this place in your book?

8. Where is the character trying to get to in this chapter?

9. Where would your character rather be at this moment?

10. Where are the places the character has been to in the past that helped to shape the personality they are exhibiting at this moment?

Note: Which two or three questions do you want to answer to later include when you write each chapter on your computer? Have them ready when you schedule two hours to input a chapter. Maybe you won't use any in this category.

Why

1. Why were things going right or wrong for the character before this incident occurred?

2. Why did it actually happen in the first place?

3. Why did your character react the way they did?

4. Why didn't anyone have a solution or answer to the problem at first?

5. Why was this situation so difficult for the character?

6. Why didn't the character see this problem coming?

7. Why would your character want to do what they're doing?

8. Why did your character become a better person through the experience?

9. Why did things end in this chapter the way they did?

Note: Which two or three questions do you want to answer to later include when you write each chapter on your computer? Have them ready when you schedule two hours to input a chapter. Maybe you won't use any in this category.

How

1. How did your character react to the worst moments?

2. How did your character feel at the worst moment?

3. How did your character react to the best moment?

4. How did your character feel at the best moment? (Always described the most intense feeling in every episode.)

5. How did your character get themselves into that situation in the first place?

6. How was a solution to the dilemma found?

7. How was the solution implemented?

8. How did they know whether the solution was working or failing?

9. How could the character have avoided the problem they got into in this chapter?

Note: Which two or three questions do you want to answer to later include when you write each chapter on your computer? Have them ready when you schedule two hours to input a chapter. Maybe you won't use any in one category.

The number of questions you answer determines the number of pages in one chapter. In fiction, chapter length differs. If you answer 5 questions, you may have five pages. If you answer 7, you'll create seven.

Sample Questions your Reader Wants to NOSE

These various "nosey" questions are made up of those that the reader would most prefer to have answered: You can substitute "your main character" for "you." Use these if they help you flush out your chapter.

1. What exactly is it that is happening to you?

2. How did you wind up in this situation in the first place?

3. Was this something you really want to do ...why?

4. Who was with you and why were they there?

5. How well did you get along with this person then?

6. What was the actual cause of this incident?

7. What was the very best that you hoped might happen during this situation or later because of it?

8. What was the worse you feared that might happen? What was the "worse case scenario" you could imagine at the time?

9. How did you feel?

10. How did you react?

11. Did your own reactions surprise you...why, or why not?

12. Was there something humorous or profound said by you or someone else during this incident?

13. Where were you when this occurred?

14. What did the place look like? Where there any particular smells" Are there any sounds unique to this place?

15. When did this happen? Or...over how long did this incident last?

16. What did you do or plan to do about this situation?

17. How did you come up with this idea?

18. How well did your plan (or plans) work out in the end?

Gripping, Compelling Chapters Need Conflict

When reading another book, have you ever been drowned in too much detail, too much dialogue that doesn't move the story forward? Today's audience wants not only easy to read, but action chapters. Be sure to include some conflict in each chapter.

Seven Human Conflicts

1. Human vs. elements (environment)

2. Human vs. nature

3. Human vs. machine

4. Human vs. time

5. Human vs. luck

6. Human vs. human

7. Human vs. self

From these seven conflicts, (maybe you can add a new one) choose one or two for a particular chapter. Show the conflict in dialogue or inner dialogue; show it in your character's behavior or language; show it in the scene of your story.

Remember, your story needs conflict for action.

Rules of Action

1. What your character imagines is more exciting than what is really happening to them. In each situation your character finds himself in, what is the best or worst that can possible happen? Get into the head and heart of your characters. One best way is to say a character's inner thoughts (put in Italics) that don't agree with his actions or dialogue with another character. See the excitement of the moment through their eyes.

2. Never let your action happen without teetering for a moment on the edge. It is the momentary uncertainty, knowing things can go either way that enhances the action. Let your reader savor the terror.

3. What is happening now is more exciting than what already happened. Present much of your story in the present tense, mainly by using dialogue. Like the movies, make your reader an eye witness. Avoid, like a disease, passive construction with linking verbs like "is," "was." Circle all of these on your first draft. Avoid too many adjectives and adverbs because they tell instead of show. Then think of ways to create more action using action verbs and interesting nouns to replace the dull, overused words. Instead of she walked slowly, say she strolled. Instead of she was sick of her job, say she hated her job. (See Special Report on Power Words at Judy's Web site)

4. Could this episode cause conflicts for the characters involved? Conflict is the confrontation between two or more opposing forces. Conflict creates a place in the story where a character cares about what he may gain or lose. How much he cares affects the conflict's power. If he has nothing to gain or lose, who cares what the outcome of the action will be?

5. When you have three or more conflicts, you have action. Today's audience wants fast-paced action, not lengthy narrative. Keep the narrative balanced with dialogue, anecdotes, and analogies.

> **Author's Tip:** Always think, "What can I write to keep the reader engaged? What is compelling about the situation, the protagonist, the hook? What does this story promise the reader?

Now that you have the format for one non-fiction, how-to chapter and one fiction chapter, you need to follow the same format for all the rest of the chapters.

> **Author's Tip:** Don't make the mistake of most emerging authors. Write the easiest chapter first. You don't have to write your chapter one first. Make it easy for you to stay motivated, so you can finish your book. A finished book is your goal. Follow one chapter's format to make all of your chapters sparkle and be easy to read. This works especially well for non-fiction.

Naturally, it's OK to put a few notes into the other chapters in their separate Word folders or files, but when you finish fully, your other chapters will practically write themselves because you know the blueprint.

Conclusion

Now that you know how to create a vital chapter, you need to also know how to pre-sell your book by knowing its "Essential Nine Not-Selling-Points." These make you ready to promote and market the day you write your last page.

Mindmapping—Another Way to Outline Your Book and Book Chapters

While some of you appreciate the lists, the sequential points in an outline, many of you prefer a creative approach to appeal to your right-brain strengths. You like the open-ended way of a mindmap. You appreciate color in branches for different points. You like the key word phrases for chapter titles. Just to let you know, your author mind mapped each chapter of this book before she wrote the details.

What is Mindmapping?

Mindmapping is a color-coded outline of main ideas, sub topics and details, printed on different colored branches connected to the center. In the center in a circle, you will list your main idea, such as your book's title. *The One-*

Minute Sales Person's mindmap would have had seven different colored vertical branches coming from that center, so details can be put on connected horizontal You could also create a new mindmap that would have your chapter's title in the middle of the page. The branches would include your intro, your middle and your end.

What are the Advantages of Mindmapping?

First, a mindmap is open-ended and open-minded. No more squeezing new "ahas" or ideas into the strict, tight form of the linear outline. You can make mistakes in your mindmaps. Imperfection leads to creativity. When you get an idea for chapter one, you can just add another branch off the main one. Mindmapping expands flexible thinking, making for better writing.

Second, mindmaps use only three to five concrete or color words on a branch. These key words help jog our memory. Under Chapter One "Attracting Passion," I added several horizontal lines that represented the content that follows. One line had "opening quote," the next one "introduction," the next one "Jerry's Story," the next "Food for Thought and Action," the next, "Passion Hot Line," the last paragraph, "practice." Plus the lead into the next chapter. These ingredients went into each chapter.

Third, mindmaps speed up your writing because you only write key phrases. When you sit down at the computer, from your color-coded map, the answers will flow naturally. If you need to fatten up your chapter, just go to your chapter file folders where you keep your other questions and answers.

Fourth, in mindmaps you see the whole related to the parts. Your thesis, chapter titles and chapter contents all flow because you answered each question your readers had. This fast-forward technique allows me to write at least two or three books each year, and makes each book more organized, more focused and clear, easier to read, and finally brings more sales because people can understand the information quickly and easily.

For a picture of a mindmap of "Your Book's Format" go to
http://www.bookcoaching.com/graphics/MINDMAP.JPG.

How Do I Create My Mindmap?

Use a large sheet of paper, at least 8 ½ by 11 inches, but I recommend a large square of butcher paper or poster board, so you can spread out and enjoy the process! Have at least six or seven colored felt-tip pens in primary and bright colors ready. When you are finished, you can tape it to your office wall, and add to it as you think of something new.

To Mindmap your Book

In the center, encircle your book title. Arrange your chapter headings, each on a different colored vertical branch, around the center in any order (you can number them later). If you can't think of a title, put a few key words. Use only one color per branch. Off each main branch, put five or so other horizontal branches of particular chapter parts.

Even though you later change your mind about the contents, this initial mindmap gives you the overall picture of what your book is and what it will share with its readers. I made several mindmaps of my *Passion* book before I settled on the best information to include.

To Mindmap Each Chapter. From the instructions above, make a new mindmap for each chapter on a separate 8 by 11 sheet. Use the four major colors for the branches and start again with your chapter title encircled in the middle of the page. You'll include:

introduction with a hook, your middle of how to's, stories, tips, case studies, and the end summary and benefit-driven last sentence inviting your reader to the next chapter.

Practice: Create your book's mindmap on a separate piece of paper

Practice: Create one chapter's mindmap on a separate piece of paper now.

Wow! You are up to speed. You have your thesis and main question to answer, your chapter working titles, your rough draft evolving with a Table of Contents, and you have questions to answer in each chapter

Market While You Write With Your Book's "Nine Essential Hot Selling Points"

It's best to know the nine "Essential Hot_Sselling Points" before you write your book, but if you have it finished already, you can still apply them. What will help your potential readers decide whether to spend their money on your book or not? These hot-selling points help pre-market and pre-sell your book.

1. Title.
2. Cover.
3. Thesis.
4. Preferred Audience.
5. Table of Contents.
6. Benefits and Features.
7. Thirty-Second "Tell-and-Sell."
8. Back Cover.
9. Introduction.

First, your potential buyers will check out your title and cover, which reflects your particular audience, then your back cover with your book's promises, testimonials, and "tell and sell" included, then the table of contents reflecting your particular audiences' needs, then the preface or introduction. These hot-selling points are all-important to your future book sales, and will help you write a better book too.

Market Each Part of Your Book as You Write It to Write Fast

If you create the "Essential Nine-Hot Selling Points," before you write a single chapter, you can include particular information that helps sell your book. You'll write compelling copy faster, because you won't write anything that doesn't belong in your book. That equates to writing your eBook or other book, publishing it, and multiplying sales faster.

Benefits of Knowing the "Nine Essential Hot-Selling Points"

- Helps you write focused, compelling copy, so you write your book fast.
- Helps you market and promote while you write, getting you completely ready to sell by the time your book is finished.
- Cuts editing time in half, also helping get your book finished quickly.
- Makes your book easy to read, cohesive, and organized.
- Helps you sell thousands of books, rather than hundreds.

Essential Hot Selling Point Number One. Titles Sell Books

A title is great if it is clever, but a clear title is always preferable. The best? A clear and clever title. A shorter title is better than a longer one. Your reader will spend only five to ten seconds on the cover. While some long titles have succeeded, usually the shorter, the better.

A title is part of your book's front cover. Busy buyers, including bookstore buyers, wholesalers, distributors and your audiences, buy mainly because of the cover. Dan Poynter, author of "Writing Non fiction," says, "The package outside sells the product inside."

Start with a working book title before you write your chapters. Include your topic, your subject and the book's benefits in the title or subtitle if possible.

Here are your ten tips for titles that sell:

1. Create impact for your title; check out print and radio ad headlines.

   Check out other authors' titles on the bookstore shelves. Your title must compel the reader to buy now. Which title grabs you? *Elder Rage* or *Care giving for Dad?*

2. Include your solution in your title.

   Does your title sell your solution? Make sure it answers the question rather than asks one. For instance, *Got Minerals?* or *Minerals: The Essential Link to Health.* Use positive language instead of negative. For instance, *Without Minerals You'll Die* can be *Minerals: The Essential Link to Health.*

3. Make it easy for readers to buy.

   Readers want a magic pill. They want to follow directions and enjoy the benefits the title promises. *The Artist's Way's* subtitle "A Spiritual Path to Higher Creativity" gives the main benefit within the title.

4. Expand your title to other books, products, seminars, and services.

   Make sure that your title will work well with the title of your presentations, articles and sales letters you'll need to promote the book. Such seminars and teleclasses titled "How to Write and Sell Your Book-Fast!" and "Seven Sure-Fire Ways to Publicize your Business" come under the umbrella "fast book writing, publishing and promoting."

5. Use original expressions–a way of expressing one idea for your book– yours alone.

   Sam Horn, author of *Tongue Fú!*, puts her special twist on defusing verbal conflict.

6. Include benefits in your subtitle if your title doesn't have any.

   Specific benefits invite sales. For instance, Marilyn and Tom Ross' *Jump Start Your Book Sales: A Money-Making Guide for Authors, Independent Publishers and Small Presses.*

7. Choose others' book covers in your field as models.

   Go to your local bookstore with five-colored felt tips pens and paper. Browse the section your book would be shelved on. Choose five book titles and covers that attract you. Photo copy or sketch those, noting the colors, design, fonts, and sizes of fonts. Add other colors you like. Place the book cover you love near your workstation to inspire you. For the final copy, use professional cover designers if possible.

8. Be outrageous with your book title.

    People do judge a book by its title. Your reader will spend only five to ten seconds on the front cover and fifteen seconds on the back cover. It must be so outstanding and catchy that it compels the reader to either buy on the spot or look further to the back cover. Take a risk. Be a bit crazy, even outlandish. Cliché's make good titles especially when you tweak them because people know them and can connect to them.

9. Be your strongest salesperson self.

    Choose the strongest words, benefits, and metaphors to move your audience to buy. Titles do sell books.

10. Include your audience in your title to give your book a slant.

    When your title isn't targeted famous authors' titles win out. Always make your title clear. Make it easy for your audience to recognize that they need your book. Your title and front cover are your book's number one sales tools. Short titles are best; say, three to six words. John Gray didn't get much attention with his book *What Your Mother Couldn't Tell You and What Your Father Didn't Know.* He shortened it to the famous, *Men are From Mars, Women are From Venus.*

An outstanding title sells books. Make sure to give this part of your book, the number one "Essential Hot-Selling Point," some time and effort.

Author's Tip: List about ten titles, and distribute them via email among friends, associates, or professionals in your field. Have them vote on the three they like best. Ask them what benefit, word, or phrase captured their interest enough to lay out money for your book. Ask them to contribute a few sample titles that would sell them. Keep the list in your computer. Revise your title many times until it's just right. Be open to brainstorming. Leave your judgment behind. Write them down, even those that you think are losers, because later, they may trigger some good ideas. This casual market research is a powerful tool. Use it for all the parts of your book, even your chapters.

Practice. Write your book's working title now to help you focus and answer your readers' questions about the topic.

Some Great Titles

The Art of Kissing sold over 60,500 over its original title of *The Art of Courtship* selling only 17, 500.

Speak and Grow Rich by Dottie Walters played on Napoleon Hill's title, *Think and Grow Rich.*

Your Erroneous Zone sold millions because many people mistook the title.

Essential Hot Selling Point Number Two: Create a Cover That People Can't Resist.

Bookstore buyers, publishers and your individual consumer buy books based on the cover alone. They give your book only a few seconds, so make your cover outstanding.

Four-color covers are a must for most books. Some new authors will write an 8½ by 11 eDocument and prefer a simple one or two-color cover.

Most books on the bookstore shelves are perfect-bound. A printer attaches the insides to the spine. These books are four-color usually and are usually a common size of 5½" by 8½" or 6" by 9". A professional book cover designer may charge you anywhere from $200 to $2500. Check out local graphic artists who charge from $50–$100 an hour, or use talent from a local graphics arts college. One local author, Sally Gary, of *San Diego Deals and Steals*, took a great picture of San Diego's port, herself. What a great cover for around $50. Imagination counts!

Color covers sell books. Use colors your audience will like and expect. Women enjoy turquoise, yellow, red and white. Business people expect blues, reds, and maroons. Red always attracts. Go to your local bookstore and browse the shelves in the area your book will fit in such as non-fiction or self-help. Choose three covers that attract you. Until your original version evolves, sketch your cover using others' ideas with colored felt-tip pens or pencils. Visit professional book cover Web sites to learn from the best such as www.fostercovers.com or MaxCovers.

Author's Tip: Inspire yourself! Put the best version of your book cover near your workstation.

Essential Hot Selling Point Number Three: Write Your Book's Thesis or Theme

Write a thesis for your non-fiction book. A thesis answers your reader's one major challenge. It's the number one benefit your book delivers. It's your book's central focus.

Knowing the thesis before you write your chapters helps keep you on track. All chapters should support it. A thesis for *Passion at Any Age* is, "Each of you has passion, it's natural, and you can unleash it through these twelve steps." In *Time Management for the Creative Person*, Lee Silver offers this thesis: "The creative person needs right brain methods to stop procrastination, get control of the clock and calendar, and free up their time and life."

Write a theme for your fiction book. A theme expresses a general truth about life without mention of characters, scene or plot. What truth about the human condition does your book offer? For example, in her book, *In Times of War: Memoirs of a World War II Nurse*, Isabelle Cook's theme is: While both sides suffer in war, love and adventure can emerge."

Essential Hot Selling Point Number Four: Know your Audience

"Everyone will want to read my book!" many writers say.

But the truth is that most potential buyers who see your book will say, "So what! Why should I read your book?

You may think everyone should read your book, but who actually will put down $15–$30 of their hard earned money to buy it? Who really needs or wants your book?

> **Author's Tip:** Don't write a single chapter of your book until you have spent time getting to know your best audience. Keep their "snap shot" beside you as you write each page.

Knowing your audience is also important for your Web site before you hire a Web master. You need to write the sales copy first, so when people do visit your site, they will have a reason to buy.

Know These Five Audiences to Write a Top Selling Book

To create a saleable book you need to know your preferred audience or audiences before you write your book. This "essential hot-selling point" helps you write focused, organized, and compelling copy your audience will appreciate and talk about.

Speaking directly to your reader on each page makes you the savvy author your readers will appreciate and respect. Solving your audience's challenge or problem creates happy customers who will spread the word about you and your book. Which audience below will want to pay $15–$40 for your book?

Which of These Five Audiences Suits your Book?

1. The Audience you Meet in the Mirror

    Authors write books because we love the ideas, the content, the skills we will share. We usually write the book for ourselves first. Have you heard, "I wrote the book I wanted to read?" Our passion for our topic can create success so long as we stay with a marketing and promotion plan for at least two years.

2. The Target Market Who Wants Answers Now.

    No, not everyone will want your book, although many authors think so. Your target audience has a common need or problem. Your product or service will solve that problem. For instance, http://www.stopyourdivorce.com's book already has an audience who wants a solution now. They are desperate at this point, and they will do anything. They will pay any price for your magic pill. They will buy on the spot.

    In just two years, this site sold 150 thousand books. The author answered the dilemmas that compelled the rejected spouses to buy now.

    Divorce often comes as a surprise, so without much time to negotiate, and because of great pain and discomfort, this audience wants a cure right now. Only after the doctor announces a serious prostate problem, do most men look for an answer. Prevention does not appeal to them. Only the doctor's wake up call prompts action.

    The narrower the target is, the more angles your book takes, the easier it is to sell.

3. The Short-Cut Time and Money Investment for a Big Payoff.

This audience wants a roadmap to where they want to go, and they want to get there *now!* This audience wants to know how to do something, such as to write a book, to make money Online, to promote their business Online or to put up a top-selling Web site. They also are looking for the least expensive way to accomplish their goals. No more money down the drain for them.

For instance, entrepreneurs searching for a short cut to finishing their books and getting them sold to quickly multiply their profits are the best audience for books about publishing, business or book promotion.

Once the book is near completion, how can authors make continuing sales that make up at least one-half of their income? Still relatively unused to promote, the Internet provides this answer, because Internet sellers encounter minimal competition.

4. The Massive Passionate Audience.

Think about your book. Is one aim to entertain and inspire?

These are the readers of the Chicken Soup series. Think about the 70 million plus sold so far, and the authors didn't even have to write the book. Full of inspirational short stores, this passionate audience responded well. The authors, however, did put on a full-blown marketing campaign for years.

Your book will have stiff competition in this category, yet the sheer volume of sales, like the 70 million who shop Wal-Mart every day, can make up for that. One client wrote a how-to book aimed at the now 70 million baby boomers out there called "Put Old on Hold." She's an inspiration herself; she looks and feels like 50.

5. The Online Audience of Millions

If you are like me, you love your book(s) and want others to benefit from reading it. But, if you are discouraged at the number of sales through traditional methods, you may want to consider the Internet.

First, when you write for Online sales, you can offer your print book electronically, now known as an eBook or eDocument. You need make only a few changes such as shortening your chapters, paragraphs and sentences. Busy people who shop Online want their information to be concise, clear, and cohesive. Likely to be skimmers, they don't need long stories to learn a point.

This audience is more than happy to download and print out chapters of your book. They will appreciate your book in 8½ by 11" form called an eDocument, or other, and think total page length up to ninety-nine acceptable.

The savvy author can make many more sales by dividing and conquering. A 15-page chapter can become a short eBook. You also have a built in promotion machine in your book, because you excerpt short pieces and articles to submit to online opt-in (no spam) ezines and top Web sites in your field.

The advantages of promoting your book via the Internet include; no telling or selling in person, no travel and more convenience, such as instant delivery and reaching greater numbers of your target audience. The author keeps all the profits and doesn't have to package and mail. His faster sales bring him marketing and promotion money, where most authors don't usually succeed. He can invest in books, seminars, coaching or teleclasses to bring him up to speed.

Every day you can reach thousands, even hundreds of thousands, using simple online promotion techniques. Here, you can sell your book through subtle forms, such as the free article or ezine. The varied online audiences, including personal growth and business audiences, want free information. When you share free information with them, your book sales will multiply fast, because in every email you send out, you include your signature file that leads people to where you sell your book. The best thing about writing and promoting for this audience is that it's all totally free.

Even the newbie or non-techie like me can benefit from writing for the online audience.

Use these "know your book audience" tips and examples to write compelling copy that will guarantee your writing adventure a true success. Your audience awaits!

> **Author's tip:** to be consistent—in 10 spaces eacy side. Not each line centered but like in a box.

> **Author's Note:** When asked about those for whom he writes, novelist John Updike once replied, "For a precocious twelve-year-old in Kansas." You can see that he knows his audience. What word pictures can you give for your audience?

Who is your particular audience? Make sure you know them, inside and out.

How old are they? Male? Female? Age? Baby boomers? Seniors? Entrepreneurial? Corporate? Are they middle or upper class? What kind of work do they do? What is their income? What do they spend discretionary time and money on? Where do they live? What books and magazines do they read? What different attitudes do the answers to these questions and others reflect?

What are their interests, hobbies, and values? What challenges do they face that they want answers to? What radio shows do they listen to? What TV programs do they watch? What events do they attend?

What organizations do they belong to? What causes do they support? Are they Internet-savvy? What kinds of sites do they visit? How many of them are out there to sell to? What do they want? Need?

Go to your library or use the Internet to research just how many people belong to your audience. Ask for the reference books that have census and other information. All agents and publishers will want this information from you.

Even if you publish this book yourself, do some market research. My research helps my clients who write books similar to mine: 45 million readers read new age books, 70 million baby boomers and 60 million seniors are out there. They buy online, too.

Advantages of Knowing and Writing for your Target Market

When you discover your preferred audience, your book will have its own slant and will stand out from the crowd. When it has more focus, although everyone won't buy it, it will sell more copies because your buyers really want your message.

You will sell more books with an angle. Think of the organizations that will want you to speak or will buy books for their members. Think of the most highly visited Web sites who will want your information. They are always looking for new content. Think of the ezines who will want a short article or tip. Your promotion can start as soon as you have your audience!

One Client's Particular Audience Challenge

One client wanted to write an eBook. Her working title was *How to Get People to Listen to You.* She felt she had a least four female audiences. The 20's, 30's, 40's and 50's. My feedback was that her audience was too broad. She needed to focus on one particular audience. Finally, she chose single women from 35 to 45. Her profile included their particular problems, concerns and interests.

It was a good start, but she needed to delineate her audience more. What does she physically look like? What magazines does she read? How does she spend her time? What organizations does she belong to? What sections of the paper does she enjoy? What kind of outdoor activities, both indoor and outdoor, does she engage in? What Web sites does she visit? How does she feel about her body, her future? What are her passions? How does her busy, hurried life style affect her communication? Does she practice a religion or consider herself on a spiritual path? What's missing in her life? What does she want? What's the reason she wants someone to listen to her? A committed relationship, marriage, companion, date?

At first, my client couldn't pin down the primary reason her audience wanted these skills. Was it to build self-esteem, be happy, peaceful, and accept who she is and what she is meant to do? Was it to be heard, loved, respected, appreciated, and above all, liked for who she was? Can you see what direction this book might take?

Could the slant the author is looking for be *How to Listen to Men and Get Them to Listen to You.* Could its benefits be a path to marriage? Committed relationship? Dating?

Notice the specific benefits of marriage and dating. Keep the outcome in mind for your audience, because that is why they buy.

> **Author's Tip:** Knowing your specific audience gives you your unique selling point.

How to Discover Your Primary Audience and Where to Locate Them

Exercise One: Write your audience profile. Include as many details from the above information as you can. What are their daily concerns? Habits? How do they spend their leisure time? What are they willing to spend money on? What are they unwilling to spend money on? When they visit a bookstore, what section do they visit? What seminars do they attend? Do they buy online?

Exercise Two: Send by mail or email a market survey to your friends and associates. What other things do they know about your audience profile? This brainstorming can save you so much time later! When you know your one preferred audience, you don't write several books under one cover; that covers too wide a range. With a slant, you make your book stand out from the crowd.

How to Write Your ebook or Other Short Book—Fast is geared primarily to professionals and small business people who want or need to write a book. They may need more credibility, want to promote their business, want to give their special gifts to clients or want a permanent revenue stream for life. Their challenges include perceived lack of time to write; they assume that it's too big a job, and they may not think of themselves as writers. This book is geared to these people primarily.

Do I have any other audiences? Of course. Retired people often want to write memoirs or a how-to book from their lifetime of experience. Yet, I focus my promotion time first on the primary audience. If I marketed this book to everyone, I would spend too much time and money shooting buckshot instead of hitting my target.

Always put your effort on one audience at a time. You'll be so much more successful and not feel overwhelmed.

Exercise Three: Now, write a personal letter to your one audience telling them why you are writing this book, what you think it will do for them (benefits), and what questions it will answer for them about the subject. If you are writing fiction, show them a scene or two and include benefits such as entertainment, laughs, and edge-of-their-seat suspense. Write less than a page.

Example for Write Your eBook or Other Short Book—Fast!

Dear Professional (coaches, speakers, writers, authors, seminar leaders, business people):

I'm writing this indispensable book because I know you want to share your unique message with thousands, rather than hundreds of readers. You want to raise the bar and create more credibility in your profession. You want continuous income you don't have to be present for. Its "Essential Nine Hot-Selling Points" will make your job easy, target your market, and market your book while you are writing it. You'll produce a great-selling book you can sell on the Internet while you sleep! And you don't even need your own Web site!

Even if you think you can't write, that it's too big a job, or it will take too much time, *How to Write Your Ebook or Other Short Book – Fast's* seven chapters are the fast lane to writing, publishing and selling more copies of your book than you ever dreamed of! It's the companion to Dan Poynter's Self-Publishing Manual.

Exercise Four: Now, take the above "dear audience letter" and amplify it for your book's sparkling introduction. Most emerging writers make the mistake of writing a long introduction all about their story. Not a good idea. Your audience wants to know what your book will do for them. This number 5 "hot-selling point" is your book's mini sales letter.

Essential Hot Selling Point Number Five: Your Sparkling Introduction

Why write an introduction? Nobody reads it anyway. Up until now, this opinion has had clout. But now, with a shorter introduction of only one page, and through the five essentials below, your introduction will become another top sales tool for your book. When people read your clear, concise personal note to them, they will buy your book on the spot!

Your Book's Introduction Includes:

1. **The hook.** Your first paragraph must compel your potential buyer to read more, so they will buy your book. Make your opener short–one sentence is best. Answer their question, "So What? Why should I buy your book?" Your opener may be a few questions about where your audience is now with their particular challenge. It may be a shocking statistic or fact, a powerful quote or a headline of a top benefit. It may be a short vignette from one of your chapters. Whatever it is, it must grab the reader's attention.

2. **The background.** Your particular audience has challenges. Describe where they are now, why they haven't succeeded and how they are uninformed in a short paragraph or two. Include a few sentences on why you wrote the book. At the end of this information, state your thesis statement, a general statement of what your book will give them.

3. **The benefits.** In the next paragraphs, keep answering the "So what?" that is inside every potential buyer's mind. Show the general benefits such as increased health, communication, finances or fortune. Show specific benefits. For instance, in "Write your eBook or Other Short Book-Fast!" create each part of your book as a sales tool, rewrite less, and publish cheaper and faster.

4. **The format.** Every non-fiction self-help book needs a format that gives your audience an idea of what they will experience ahead. They have already looked at the Table of Contents that gives them a general format and direction. In your introduction, you need to say what will happen in each chapter, such as the sections or headlines. This includes the how-to's, the stories, and the tips.

5. **The last sentence.** Invite your reader into the text of your book. Entice them once again with an enthusiastic "read on." In one of my writing books I used this last line, "You've been waiting too long to share your unique message. Read on and apply all the simple steps I give to make you a successful author."

Now that you've written a sparkling introduction, you have helped your potential buyer to decide to take out their wallet and purchase your book. You've also created a blue print for yourself to guide you through writing the chapters. Just remember, more important than your book's insides, the introduction may need three to five edits or more.

Essential Hot Selling Point Number Six: Your Table of Contents Created from your Chapter Titles

Chapter titles also pre-sell your book. People like to thumb through the table to see what appeals to them. They like original, clever, and branded chapter titles. Branding your chapter titles is like branding your book title or your business name and purpose. Branding is one way to show yourself as the savvy expert in your field.

Even within your chapters, you can brand yourself again with either your name or metaphor for tips or how-to's. For instance in a book, "Passion At Any Age" I originally called one chapter "Getting Support." To get more creative and brand myself as the "passion" coach, I replaced that title and all the others with one form of the word "passion." That chapter's title turned out to be "Passionate Support." For more branding to make my book stand out from the crowd, within each chapter, I put tips in a box periodically throughout the chapter, calling them, "Passion Hot Tips."

Think about Donald Trump. He puts his name first in every book he writes.

Remember the "One-Minute" brand in *The One-Minute Sales Person*? This metaphor became a brand for Spencer, who used it in each chapter title. Other copy-cats used the term for seminars and other books such as *The One-Minute Nurse*.

Your chapter titles become the table of contents for your book. You can make them dramatic and branded when you put a little thought into them. It's definitely worth your time.

Essential Hot Selling Point Number Seven: Benefits and Features

Entrepreneurs know their business. They know their product and their service. Many of them write creative Web sites, but, they are not as adept at writing their own promotional copy.

It's not the book, it's the hook! It's not the beautiful Web site; it's the one with benefit-driven headlines that lead your visitor straight to your sales message. What you say outside on your book's cover matters. What you say about your service on your Web site must be infinitely more powerful than your pleasing personality or features of the book, such as its page numbers, its ten tips.

Know the Difference between Benefits and Features

Always promote with benefits over features. Benefits show the value of your products. They solve your particular audience's problem! They show your clients and customers outcomes they will gain after they read your book. Some common benefits include: more money, less trouble, more time, less stress, desirable relationships, less drama and trauma, more zest and energy, and less fatigue.

Start your Benefit List Today

Write down a list of five to ten benefits for each product and service. Your clients and customers can't make an informed decision to buy if they don't have enough information. The information that they want is "What's in it for me?" Include general benefits such as "become financially independent," and explain what that looks or feels like. Earn $4000 income each month or more, so you can take that long needed vacation, pay your child's college tuition, or get that new car you've waited so long for.

Show your customer how he/she will feel after buying your book. For instance, after you read this, you'll look and feel ten years younger without a face-lift. Include some of your personality in your promotion copy. "My book is less than the price of a good dinner, with wine, of course!" The skills in it will serve you every day for as many times as you choose to duplicate your results.

Always answer your customers, "Why should I buy your book or service?" Sharing the strong benefits that help them solve their problem is important. Benefits sell.

Market Survey your Associates for Help

Since you are not a natural at this game, email your benefit words and phrases to associates and friends, asking them what top three benefits will make them pay your book's price? Maybe they can vote "1-5" for your best five or so benefits.

Keep this list in a file within your book's promotion folder to help keep it growing. You will need this again when you write your book's sales letter for email promotion and on your Web site. The biggest mistake authors make is to not write powerful sales messages to give their readers reasons to choose their book.

Essential Hot Selling Point Number Eight: The Thirty-Second Tell-and-Sell

How would you like to have countless people clamoring for your book before it's even released?

Most people wait until their book is finished before they think about marketing it. What a shame!

Maybe you've said, "My book is about...." You mention the subject, explain the how, and tell a story or two. If the person is kind, he may hear a bit of your story, but most people today, including your reader, agent, publisher, bookseller or an organization you may want to speak for, all want concise and precise information, and they want it fast! Remember your potential buyer as thinking, "So what?" Why should I read this book?"

When you know your sizzling title, unique selling point, preferred audience and benefits before you put words to paper, you have a billboard that can quickly convince your audience to want to read your book.

Your Book's "Tell-and-Sell"

Write a thirty to sixty-second "tell-and-sell." This is also your elevator speech, your networking group blurb.

You only have a few seconds to impress your potential buyer. Include your title, a few benefits and the audience. Use sound bites to grab attention. *Write your Print and eBook—Fast* shows professionals how to shortcut each step of writing, publishing, and promoting a saleable short book.

Include a sound bite that grabs attention, such as "It will do more for you than instant cappuccino." You may also want to compare your book to a successful one such as *How to Write Your Ebook or Other Short Book—Fast!* takes up where Dan Poynter's "Self-Publishing Manual." leaves off.

Sample "Tell-and-Sells"

1. *Doghouse to Dollhouse for Dollars* helps investors find, buy, transform, and sell fixers for higher profits.

2. *How to Write Your Ebook or Other Short Book—Fast!* shows small business owners and professionals how to short cut each step of writing, publishing and promoting a saleable short book.

Add a Sound Bite

At the end of your short blurb, add a possible sound bite that your buyers can connect to, such as a comparison to a book like yours by a famous name, already a great seller. Your buyers, which include booksellers, distributors, wholesalers, agents, corporations, internet publishers or individuals, will want your book because it is in good company.

For *How to Write Your Ebook or Other Short Book—Fast!* I compared my book to Dan: Dan Poynter's *The Self Publishing Manual.* This book takes up where Dan's book left off showing you the "fast-forward" chapter writing technique and the pre-marketing know-how of the "hot selling points."

Without your "Thirty-Second Tell-and-Sell" that strongly states the main benefit, audience, and what makes your product unique, you will bore your visitor and lose that attention you need to entice him or her to take out their wallets and pay you on the spot. The "Tell-and-Sell" is the shortest sales letter you will write. You can also use this at any business meeting or appointment where you only have a few seconds to impress.

When you know your sizzling title, unique selling point, preferred audience and benefits, you are on your way to sales—many sales.

Author's Tip: Your "Tell-and-Sell" must be clear, compact, compelling and commercial. Be prepared to write five to fifteen versions until the best one emerges.

Test your Tell-and-Sell with an email Market Survey

Before you settle on your "Tell-and-Sell," email four or five versions to your friends to vote on. Usually, a "1" vote is low, and a "10" vote is high. They will more likely respond to some benefit that is visual, or on one their emotions connect with. They also like sound bites, and you would be wise to compare your book to some famous person's book in your field. Here's your format:

1. Name the book (use branding pizzazz).

2. Name the audience that your product best serves.

3. Show how your product will solve your audiences' problem.

Put these together with a clever sound bite that will help your potential buyer to remember you, and you have a compelling "Tell-and-Sell."

Example: *How to Write Your Ebook or Other Short Book—Fast!*

1. Repeat the title *How to Write Your Ebook or Other Short Book—Fast!*

2. Shows small business people who want to make money quickly and easily. (Audience)

3. Short cuts to write each chapter title and rest of the book with few edits to produce, publish, and promote a salable book in less than 30 days. (Benefits)

Add a possible sound bite:

It's the perfect companion to, and takes off from, Poynter's *Self Publishing Manual.*

The Other Benefits of Knowing your "Tell-and-Sell"

If you know your "tell-and-sell" before you write your Web site, you'll write a far more compelling home page and sales letter for each product or service you sell. Your potential customer deserves this concise, precise information that will make them want to keep learning more about your product or service.

The Big Benefits?

If you know your "tell-and-sell" before you write your book, you'll be marketing while you write, because you will write your book from your audience's needs. Your book will much improved, because you will write more organized and focused copy. Every chapter will prove your "tell-and-sell." You'll answer all of your audience's questions. You will also write faster because with focus and my "Fast-Forward" writing technique in Chapter Seven, you'll need far less edits and rewrites.

Essential Hot-Selling Point Number Nine: Writing Your Back Cover Copy

Many authors of eBooks or other short books miss sales because they either take little time with the back cover information, or they skip it altogether.

One reason authors don't create dynamic back covers is because they don't realize the importance of the "Essential Hot Selling Points" that need to be addressed before they write their book. Your potential buyer will spend only fifteen seconds or so on the back cover. Make sure you fill it with potent ad copy and testimonials. These can come directly from your "tell-and-sell" statement.

> **Authors Tip:** Find a book similar to yours with a back cover that appeals to you, and use it as your model. Include a lot of white space and fonts that are at least size 12, so it's easy to read. What a turn off to your potential buyers when they can't easily read it. Even seasoned writers make this mistake. After you create one back cover, count its words, and then reduce them to keep ad copy to seventy words or less for a 5 ½" by 8 ½" or 6" by 9" cover.

Parts of the Self-Help Back Cover

Practice. On a separate piece of paper, mock up your back cover based on the models below.

1. **Category:** psychology/non-fiction/self-help/health? Go to your bookstore to discover where you book might fit. The category is usually placed in the top left side.

2. **Headline:** This first phrase on the back of the book must be catchy to get the reader to read on. Include benefits. For example, "Imagine Thou-

sands Reading your Book Next Month!" on the back cover of *Write your eBook or Other Short Book Fast.* or "What's So Tough About Writing?" on Richard Lederer's back cover of *The Write Way.* Don't put your title at the top of the back cover because your buyer has already seen it on the front cover.

3. **Ad Copy:** What the book is about, sales copy/description. For example, "Most people don't write a book, because they think it will take too long, take too much effort, not sell well, and they don't think of themselves as writers. Untrue! With the "fast-forward" technique and the essential "hot-selling points," you can write a salable book in less than a month!

4. **Promises and Benefits:** Use 3-5 bullets for example:

    – Write focused, compelling, and targeted copy.

    – Catapult your clients and monthly profits.

    – Sell thousands of books even without a Web site.

    – Enjoy immediate profits through Internet marketing.

    – Finish each chapter fast—to get your book self-published fast.

5. **Testimonials**—They sell more copies than anything else. Learn how to contact influential people before your book is published! (See eBook *How to Get Testimonials from the Rich and Famous"* Include these: important professionals in your my field, a famous or local media person, celebrities interested in your field, and a "man-on-the-street." Samples below:

"This is not a book on how to write. It is a book on how to get it written. It is full of the shortcuts, experiences and tips only an insider could know. Whether you are working on an eBook or a pBook, you will find Judy Cullins' wisdom invaluable."

Dan Poynter,
author of *The Self Publishing Manual and Writing Non-Fiction*

"Whoever said 'Fifty percent of writing is getting the first word on a blank piece of paper' should have had Judy Cullins' book! It's inspiring and practical, an unbeatable combination. *Write Your eBook or Other Short Book –Fast!* offers checklists, tips, tricks and the encouragement you need to get your book out of your head and onto the shelves. If you've ever thought of writing a book or even written one but want to improve the process, get this book."

Mary Westheimer,
CEO, BookZone.com

"Save yourself from headaches, disappointments, and money down the drain. Read *Write Your eBook or Other Short Book-Fast!* before you write another word. Judy puts you on the fastest track to publishing success."

> Marcia Reynolds, M.A., M.Ed.
> Past president of the International Coach Federation
> Author of How to Outsmart Your Brain, www.covisioner.com

"Want to make money while you sleep? Ebooks are in and anyone can write them—particularly if you sit at the feet of someone who has gone before you. Get this book and get the secrets. Then write one of your own."

> Joe Vitale, author of the best selling eBook Hypnotic Writing

Author's Note: You can't have too many testimonials. Put the rest on the page after your book's title page. And, if you don't have much room on the back cover, be sure to include the testimonials. They are a big reason people buy your book.

Elder Rage Author on Her Way to a Best Seller – All Through Testimonials

While it took her nine months, Jacqueline Marcell, author of Elder Rage, got 44 glowing testimonials from celebrities like Regis Philbin, Hugh Downs, Ed Asner, Dr. Dean Edell, Johns Hopkins Memory Clinic, Duke University, and two Senators. Is she selling books? You bet! Her photo story landed on the April, 2001 cover of AARP's BULLETIN, distributed to over 22 million. She had to quickly print an extra 25,000 books to meet the instant demand. She's now a sought after speaker on eldercare awareness. See:.ElderRage.com.

6. **Author's Bio:** Make this short on the back cover. If you need to write more, place it on the inside of the back cover. For example, 20-year bookcoach Judy Cullins, M.A loves to help people write, publish, and promote their saleable books to get well known, make good income, and help their audiences. So far 55 clients published with her help.

7. **Closing:** What your audience has and your book's benefits to help them achieve their goal. For example in this book, "People need your unique message and expertise. This book supplies the how-to's to make your book a great seller. So be encouraged and start writing!"

Sample Back Cover: *Write your eBook or Other Short Book–Fast!*

Category: writing/self-publishing/reference/inspiration

Headline: Imagine Thousands Reading Your Book This Month!

What the book is about / sales copy / description:

Most people don't write a book because they think it will take too long, take too much effort, they aren't writers, or it won't sell. Untrue! Using tested short cuts, essential "hot selling points," step-by-step methods, and the "fast-forward technique," you'll be an author in less than a month. And, you'll sell far more books!

Benefits:

- Write focused, compelling, and targeted copy.
- Catapult your clients and monthly profits.
- Sell thousands of books even without a web site .

Testimonials:

"This is not a book on how to write. It is a book on how to get it written. It is full of the shortcuts, experiences and tips only an insider could know. Whether you are working on an eBook or a pBook, you will find Judy Cullins' wisdom invaluable."

Dan Poynter,
The Self-Publishing Manual and *Writing Non-Fiction.*
http://ParaPublishing.com

"Save yourself from headaches, disappointments, and money down the drain. Read *Write Your eBook or Other Short Book-Fast!* before you write another word. Judy puts you on the fastest track to publishing success."

Marcia Reynolds, M.A., M.Ed.
Past president of the International Coach Federation
Author of *How to Outsmart Your Brain*
http://www.covisioner.com

"Whoever said 'Fifty percent of writing is getting the first word on a blank piece of paper' should have had Judy Cullins' book! It's inspiring and practical, an unbeatable combination. *Write Your eBook or Other Short Book –Fast!* offers checklists, tips, tricks and the encouragement you need to get your book out of your head and onto the shelves. If you've ever thought of writing a book or even written one but want to improve the process, get this book."

Mary Westheimer, CEO, BookZone.com

8. Author's Bio: 20-year bookcoach Judy Cullins, M.A loves to help people write, publish, and promote their saleable books to get well known, make good income, and help their audiences. So far 55 clients published with her help.

Closing: People need your unique information and expertise. This book supplies the how-to's to make your book a great seller. So be encouraged and start writing–fast!

Imagine Thousands Reading Your Book Next Month

Want to brand your business with a book? Want to write a book so focused, compelling and well organized, it will be a top seller? Want to catapult passive book sales each month?

If you said yes, get help from this book that takes up where Dan Poynter left off. Write easy to read chapters using Judy's chapter format blueprint "fast-forward writing technique." Know your book's Essential Nine Hot-Selling Points" before you write a chapter, so your book pre-sells itself and you can hit the ground running for immediate sales–thousands of books, even without a Web site.

Testimonials:

"This is not a book on how to write. It is a book on how to get it written. It is full of the shortcuts, experiences and tips only an insider could know. Whether you are working on an eBook or a pBook, you will find Judy Cullins' wisdom invaluable."

Dan Poynter,
The Self-Publishing Manual and Writing Non-Fiction.

"Save yourself from headaches, disappointments, and money down the drain. Read Write Your eBook or Other Short Book-Fast! before you write another word. Judy puts you on the fastest track to publishing success."

Marcia Reynolds, M.A., M.Ed.
Past president of the International Coach Federation
Author of How to Outsmart Your Brain

"Whoever said 'Fifty percent of writing is getting the first word on a blank piece of paper' should have had Judy Cullins' book! It's inspiring and practical, an unbeatable combination. Write Your eBook or Other Short Book—Fast! offers checklists, tips, tricks and the encouragement you need to get your book out of your head and onto the shelves. If you've ever thought of writing a book or even written one but want to improve the process, get this book."

Mary Westheimer, CEO, BookZone.com

Bio: Judy Cullins, 20-year book coach is an author's advocate-to save you mistake time and money. She offers author support through her free ezines, teleclasses, small group coaching groups and one-on-one phone and email coaching via www.bookcoaching.com.

People need your unique information and expertise. This book supplies the how-to's to make your book a great seller. So be encouraged and start writing–fast!

$15.95   price   **ISBN**

Which Way to Publish is Best for You?

You have a dream—to write a useful, entertaining, and saleable book. As an "authors' advocate," I want to make your book dream a reality rather than a fantasy. Many traditional publishing myths lead authors to an unlikelihood of success. Following these myths cost authors much time, money, and effort, bringing lasting discouragement. Larger losses yet include many really good books sitting in storage spaces unread.

The Tradition Publishing Approach—and The Myths

Myth 1. Publishers will promote your book.

Reality. Most first time authors think the publisher will take his book to the best-seller list. Unless you are famous, with a great track record of 50,000 sales a year, your book and its promotion is delegated to the publisher's intern, who handles your book and 15 others. Their attention on your book will be limited, perhaps to a few months. Your book might get distributed to the bookstores, but it will only be on the bookshelves for three months unless, you as the author, promotes it.

Mary Mitchell's Story

Author, *The Complete Idiot's Guide to Etiquette, Dear Ms. Demeanor: The Young Person's guide to Handling Any Social Situation With Confidence and Grace, The Complete Idiot's Guide to Business Etiquette* and more.

"I will tell you that, sadly, publishing as most of us envisioned, is a dinosaur. I was very fortunate to have been approached by two major corporations for spokesperson assignments. Those assignments promoted my books in ways authors only pray for these days. Without those tours, my books might have died on the vine like so many other worthy titles have.

I remember feeling so disheartened when I learned that most of the publicity effort for my first book was on my shoulders. After all that work, authors find our selves at the mercy of a lumbering publicity machine, with virtually no control or support from our publishers. I suppose that's OK if you get a 6-figure advance. I don't know too many people who've arrived at that level.

Right now I'm finishing a booklet that addresses the most frequently asked questions from my seminars. I'm publishing it myself, with Judy Cullins' help, and wouldn't do it any other way - even though I'm reasonably sure I could find a publisher.

After putting in so much time and effort to do a book, there is comfort in having some measure of control in its distribution. Not to mention the added financial gains."

Author's Note: Remember, no one sells your book, but you—not your agent, your publisher, your wholesaler, your distributor or the bookstore.

It follows that authors need to update their marketing skills and follow the track of a successful self-publisher. Choose what you love and will do. Speak? Then schedule 4-6 talks each month. Write? Then learn how to write a "tell-and-sell," a five- to seven-line ad for ezines, a short sales letter for email promotion, a longer sales letter to put on your web site from a home page benefit driven headline and link.

Myth 2. To be a respected author, you must invest thousands of hours of time writing your full-length book.

Reality. Today people want concise, useful information. They want information fast and conveniently. You don't have to write a 200-page book. You can write a short book, and you can write your print and eBook at the same time. You simply create two Word files, and make your eBook up to 100 pages, and your print book slightly longer. When you put your full intention and attention into writing a short book (thirty to one hundred pages) you can get it finished in less than a month. This page count (thirty to one hundred) is the ideal size for eBooks.

Take already prepared speeches and articles, and expand them into a short book. Combine your stories with short tip lists. Remember, if you write a page a day, you'll have 365 pages at the end of the year. I recommend that you get at least 3 books out of those pages.

Myth 3. You must spend thousands on your book to get it published, $5,000 to $10,000 just for printing!

Reality. Traditional printing requires the author to print over 3 thousand books for reasonable discounts like $1 or $2 for a 130-page book. That is a lot of books unless you have already pre-sold them! That's a lot of money—up to $10,000, even more. Such a large outlay depletes your cash flow that you need for book promotion. You may not sell that many unless you are a good promoter. With such a large inventory, you may have to rent a storage unit. That's extra money. You may be left with a garage full of books.

Most emerging authors don't realize that publishers, like agents, choose only 1-2% of submissions from non-famous, non best-selling authors. The odds are slim, aren't they?

Another thing you may not know is that these publishers are more likely to look at your book after you have printed and sold ten thousand copies. That makes the following information even more useful.

Myth 4. Bookstores are the best places to sell books.

Reality. When authors think of distributing their book they think bookstore. Yet, according to John Kremer, book marketing expert and author of *1001 Ways to Market Your Book,* who switched distributors because of problems, said, "I'm glad I don't rely on retail bookstore sales for my income. But it will be nice to get that icing on the cake into my cash flow again."

John sells books from non traditional marketing strategies; his Web site, his ezine which offers tips and products and seminars, bulk sales to organizations, catalogues, specialty stores, foreign markets and back of the room sales. Because he is a recognized name, he may get his book cover side out on bookstore shelves, making it easier for browsers to buy. But when you are an unknown author, only your book's spine will show, even if it does make it to the bookstore. After two or three months of initial placement, your book will fade away unless you put ongoing effort into promotional materials to send your potential customers to the bookstores. This traditional marketing and promotion takes a lot of time, money and frustration because it nets rather small results.

In one book coaching session, a new client thought he wanted to sell to the bookstores. I asked him who his particular audience was. He said business people. What kind of business people? Do these people actually go to the bookstore for a business book? Or, will they be more likely to visit a particular business Web site for specific kinds of business books? Or, do they subscribe to a no-spam opt-in ezine about business, where smart authors submit articles to promote their books? Most people don't go into a bookstore looking for your book.

Did You Know This About Brick and Mortar Bookstores?

- Seventy percent of US adults haven't been in a bookstore in the last five years.

- Bookstores sell only forty-five percent of all books sold.

- Bookstores return non-sold books and deduct them from the author's royalties.

- Bookstores will take ninety days, even a year or more to pay you for your total book sales.

- Bookstores only order two or three copies at a time, because of limited shelf space.

Why the big push to get a wholesaler or distributor, to get bookstore distribution? These people represent so many other people; don't you wonder how much attention your book will receive? These people, as well as bookstores, extract healthy fees of up to fifty percent of the retail price of your book. That leaves a small profit for the author, and remember; the distributors and wholesales don't promote your book.

One author, after her distributor went belly up and she lost $160,000, said she would rather have more control over her priceless children's books. She distributes them all herself now, through various venues that suit her personality, including community fairs. Authors spend long hours and a small fortune chasing the improbable, when the "golden egg" of self-publishing and self-promoting is right in front of them! In my opinion, I'd sell my books everywhere except the brick and mortar bookstore!

What Should Authors Do to Promote Their Books?

One client's health book sold hundreds of copies after a columnist wrote about his book in a daily paper. With coaching, he wrote the press release. He contacted the columnist himself. Like so many authors out there, he didn't pay attention to why this succeeded. It succeeded because of his effort. Even with this proven process, the author decided he wanted to just "try something else out." Other people could do it for him. He took more expensive seminars, bought into the shopping channel, showcased his book in Europe, bought an ad in a radio magazine and bought a fax list of 700 national media, all at big expense. To update this story, this talented health author has moved on to weight loss products. He didn't really have a focused plan or promotion activities, did he?

> **Author's Tip:** Create a definite marketing plan with only three or four parts. Don't shotgun your promotion efforts. (See Book Marketing Report-Launch and First Year)

First, put a money goal out. For instance, I count the total Web sales that include selling books and coaching. My ten eBooks are my business card. They attract at least ten new clients a month to me, enabling me to maintain a client base of at least twenty per month at all times. So, if you only have a book and not a business except your book, you will count book sales. Your goal could be a book a day, or $2000 a month from books sales. When you shoot for an optimistic goal, you show intention to make money for your effort. You can also know your realistic goal, and be happy when it happens.

Second, know who your audience is, where they go to buy books. Do they shop on the Internet? Books are still the number one product people buy on the Net. Include your general or business online audience as well. These people have money and are looking for your topic, especially if it is how-to or self-help.

Third, name the actual promotion actions and dollars. For instance, will you speak? What groups? Will you do talk or radio shows? What shows? Will you travel? Will you do book signings? Will you guest speak at a teleclass? Put an estimated time and money next to this list, so you see where you spin your wheels or where you make impact. Will you market on the Internet? If you don't know how, will you subscribe to opt-in ezines like my "Business Tip of the Month" that introduces small business people to easier and cheaper marketing and promotion? Will you check out teleclasses by a qualified coach on book Internet marketing? Will you read ebooks or other short books on this topic? How will you get started?

Personalities play a big role. Bashful or behind-the-scenes people may do better on the Internet with "writing-promotion." Speakers will like "speaking-promotion." Plan your promotional efforts according to your personality and your willingness to follow through with either style of promotion. In addition, if you're smart, you'll do what works in traditional promotion, as well as what works in online promotion.

Caution: Think about the effort and time that each promotion takes. You can short cut your efforts when you give the Internet a chance; your books or services will face almost no competition there.

> **Author's Tips:** If you do "speaking-promotion," start with your local market first; then, your city, the cities near you, and finally, your whole state. Do book signings, talks, talk shows and seminars that are close to home. You may want to send out press releases for a talk you give that relates to your book. Usually, the local businesses and media support local authors. Think of the disadvantages of travel: money spent, money lost by time spent on travel, and wear and tear on you.

If you can write (you are writing a book, aren't you?), I highly recommend that you extract excerpts, short articles and tips, and submit them; not only to online spam-free ezines and top websites who want your articles, but also submit a tip or list to the print media. They are more likely to publish a short how-to article that than a press release about your book. Those usually get pitched into the round files unless you are famous. Never submit to the book editor. Most of the bigger print media papers only support the big publishing houses and already well-known authors. Instead, send your tips to the section of the paper that relates to your book.

Myth 5. You need an agent to get your book accepted by publishers.

Reality. While agents are useful to connect you to publishers, like publishers, they primarily accept books from established, best-selling authors with marketing know-how. They accept about one to two percent of submissions from new authors. Except for small publishers, they may expect you to put money into your marketing, in addition to taking an active part in the marketing.

When agents do connect you with a publisher, the publisher will give you a book tour, which may or may not be successful. It depends on how you promote it through the media, and whether you offer book talks and seminars along with your book signings. It depends on all the promotion materials, such as flyers, cards, and networking with "contacts influential." All of your book signing expenses are charged against the sale of your books, and remember, after the agents' fifteen percent, the bookstores' forty percent and the distributors' charges, your $15 book may only bring you $2.

> **Author's Tip:** If your agent/publisher deal can't make at least ten times as many sales as you do, it is wiser to publish and promote your book, yourself!

What do Agents Want?

One notable agent with fifty top clients told me at a face-to-face appointment that he liked my title, he liked the writing, and he appreciated my book marketing know-how. He wanted to take me, but he told me that I needed to put up $50,000, even though I had written a powerful marketing plan to accompany my book proposal (taking six months to write). I was unknown, and agents want a sure bet. If I had $50,000 to put up for marketing, I wouldn't need an agent, would I?

However, if clients want to take the traditional path, I refer them to short eBooks on my Web site: *How to Write a Query* and *How to Write a One-Page Book Proposal*. You may also want *Your Book's Marketing Plan—Launch and First Year and Beyond*.

One Author's Agent Nightmare

One author thought he had made the big time. At a large New Age expo, he displayed some of his self-published books on a table. An agent happened by, got the book, read it that night, and called him the next day. A whirlwind courtship took place with the eight top publishing houses. He flew to New York. The bidding reached $250,000. He was in Nirvana. After the deal, he did the book tours, signings and seminars around the country.

While he did sell books, sales were disappointing. A second mortgage on his house barely covered his expenses. While the advance looked fantastic, only a small amount was advanced at a time, and was paid against book sales.

Following his heart, the author decided to write another book, a common mistake most emerging authors make. After researching and writing this one for two years, this author submitted it to his agent/publisher. After some time, they declared they didn't want it. Talk about disappointment! Two years had gone by without much income. Now, the author had more printing costs for 5000 copies of the second book, more expenses, less cash flow. What did he do? He quit promoting his books and quit speaking about them. Disillusioned with the big boys, he did give a few seminars, but to make a living, he switched his efforts to house painting, hiring a great team to support him. His dream of being a big time successful author had become a nightmare.

> **Author's Tip:** Research outside the box. The myths above are just myths. Take a reality check. Stop wasting your valuable time and money. Like Dorothy in *The Wonderful Wizard of Oz,* your pot of gold may be right in your own back yard. As an author, you have the passion, the "know-how" and the information. You just need to take real baby steps to get your self-published book launched and selling well.

But I can't afford to write a book...

Many aspiring authors say this. When I caught myself using this excuse, I started a book bank account. When it reached $3500, I knew I could apply some of it to my updated Web site, learn from low-cost computer and Internet techie assistants, and publish primarily in eBook format.

> **Author's Tip:** Take the frugal road, as I have. Use your imagination and cleverness to get your book published. Start small. Write an ebook first; no printing bills, little formatting. Use graphic artist students for your cover. Use savvy high school and college students who have expertise in word processing and the Internet. These assistants make you look professional and much larger than a one-person show. Trade services with another professional, such as editing for coaching.

The Independent Publishing Game

You really don't need a traditional publisher or printer today.

Your options have expanded. Dan Poynter, author of *The Self Publishing Manual,* has paved the way for all of us to put out a professional-looking book more easily and less expensively than with traditional methods. Self-publishing has gained respect, because print books created this way look as professional as any others in the book store. Self-publishing is fairly easy with a little help from professionals. You only need to print a small run of approximately 200 units.

Author's Note: I recommend you print only what you can sell in three months. That leaves more money to put into marketing/promotion, the only activities that bring you sales. (Marketing means the plan, and promotion means the action). What good is a deep printing discount if you don't sell the lot?

Benefits of Print on Demand: You...

- Finish your project in half the time, even less.
- Need print only the copies you will sell, so you need less money.
- Bypass the middleman and publish straight from the disc.
- Have no unsold inventory in storage.
- Spend little, keeping your cash flow going.
- Print only the copies you need for reviews or to sell.
- Can sell your books before you even print them.
- Can update your book faster.
- Do not have to worry about your title going out of print.

For example, for two hundred copies of a 130-page book at $2.40, would be only $480 outlay. Having a professional book in your hands in such a short time to sell sooner creates an ongoing source of money that you can spend on promotion.

Author's Tip: Do what you do best, and hire the rest. Or, to spend less, some entrepreneurs use the barter system, trading one service for another. It works if you are willing, and trust is established.

Author's Recommendation: If you already have your PDF files ready and only want your book printed, the company I recommend is Deharts.com. They have done a great job for many of my clients. While some major POD publishers can get a beginner's book printed and up on their Web site, the author still has to promote. And, not all of these are equal. Be sure to read the small print so you know what you will pay for, and how much control you will have. If you are willing to treat your book like a business, be willing to promote it, make more money on it, and have more control, I can also recommend yowbooks.com. They did four eBook formats and a POD version of my book to put on Amazon.com.

Author's Tips on Book Promotion: Many emerging authors feel that it's a drawback to have to market and promote their books. Yet, you can learn skills, such as the sixty-second "tell-and-sell," the promotional article or power press release and the sales letter for your Web site from an already successful author-coach. See chapter three of this book for the "tell-and-sell" samples, and check out *Ten Non-Techie Ways to Market your Book Online* for other ways to promote your book. Reading books like these will give you the step-by-step skills to acquire, as well as an overview how book promotion works so well Online. Remember that traditional promotion services, such as publicity cost a thousands a month if you use a professional, and they can't guarantee you book sales, either.

When you have learned how to talk about your book in a few sentences, a few paragraphs and in a longer sales letter, you can either speak or write to promote your book. Even if you spend $1000 for coaching, editing and printing, you'll still be able to realize a larger profit than you will through the traditional publishing route.

You, the author, need to decide what publishing path is best for you. Make sure it's a profitable one. In the meantime, you need to pay attention to how you organize your book's folders and files. Without organization, you can spend many wasted hours looking for a particular piece of the whole. Check out the next chapter to see how to save time and money with book organizing.

Organize Your Book Before You Write It

If your book is important to you, you need to be able to find the parts that go into it when you need them. Plan ahead to either keep all of your book's parts in a file (on the computer and in hard copy), or in a huge three-hole binder with various sections.

Organize before your write chapter one!

Stop Piling and Start Filing

Maybe you're a stacker (horizontal multiple piles), a stuffer (look organized, but can't find things), a spreader (spread one pile to another place, then another), a slinger (undecided, you sling into a place behind closed doors). Did you know that each of us spends over 150 hours a year looking for important papers? These old habits die hard, but with the following "how-to's," you should be master of your book's parts in no time.

> **Author's guarantee:** You can find any part of your book within two minutes when you find a special place for each important paper.

For each piece of research, quotes and ideas that you want to file in hard copy:

- Put only one category/heading at the top.
- Write on one side of the paper only, one subject for one page.
- Use the 8 ½ by 11" format to save your notes and research on. Stop losing pieces of good material. Just tape them to the standard size paper to file.
- Put each part in its corresponding file name/folder in alphabetical order.

How many files do you need?

First, you will need a book folder to include front and back matter, chapter files, and other related information. Second, you will need a promotion/marketing folder. Third, you will need a business folder for your independent publishing information

Before you start writing, have them handy. Buy files or boxes that can hold manila folders and all of your notes and clippings in the 8 ½ by 11 size. Keep other versions in folders in Word on your computer. Whenever you see something; a book title, a quote, an article that relates to your book, a tip from an eMagazine, pop it into the proper file within the proper folder. (See file names below)

> **Author's Note:** Keep every piece of important paper vertical. If you take notes or jot down a great quote, make sure it gets taped or stapled to an 8 ½ by 11-inch paper, on one side of the paper only, so it is easy to file in a category. When you take different notes on one page, or allow your scraps of brilliance to get into the horizontal piles, one of those great ideas will get lost. Along with twenty percent of your other important papers, make your book the number one priority in your life. Give each paper a special place in your files to assure you can write your book fast!

In Your Hard Copy Book File

Fill one box or file with manila folders. Arrange and label the folders alphabetically or by parts such as "Front Matter" which includes such parts as the Title Page, Table of Contents, Testimonials, and Acknowledgements. Next, a section with your Chapters, One through the end, and within each, you will put your research, articles, partially written chapter, and questions you want to answer for each chapter. Put a color divider before each section. You will also have a "Back Matter" section.

Sample Files for your Hard Copy or Computer Folders

- Talks you create on your topic.
- Articles you wrote that may transfer into chapters.
- The " Essential Nine Hot-Selling-Points" (see Chapter Three).
- The Book's Audience.

- The Book's Introduction in Five Steps.
- The Book's "Tell and Sell".
- The Table of Contents.
- Mentions (quotes from authors with their contact information).
- Back cover (include good samples, your rough drafts).
- Front cover/title (include a list of your five best).

Back Matter

- Bibliography.
- Index—need this to sell to libraries.
- Resources/Appendix.
- Glossary.
- Author's bio/photo (inside print back cover).
- Book Order Page.

Front Matter

- Copyright page (ISBN, DOI, LCCN).
- Table of Contents.
- Other Books by Author.
- Testimonials.
- Acknowledgements.
- Foreword (only from famous person).
- Title Page.
- Introduction.
- Dedication.

Market While You Write Files

"Contacts Influential"—Create a list of 25 contacts for peer reviews/testimonials. These people help sell your books. Include media in your area, celebrities that have an interest in your topic, man/woman on the street, and others who know your service or book. Keep them in a file on your computer in the book promotion folder

In Each Chapter File

Include working title, chapter hook and intro, page numbers, notes, stories, how-to's, quotes, sidebars, exercises, and tips.

Create a format for each chapter. (See Chapter Seven)

In Your Marketing/Promotion File

- Marketing plan—launch and lifetime.
- Query/One-page book proposal if you seek an agent.
- Professional "One-Sheet" programs/seminars/talks if a speaker.
- Email database in group categories.
- Your Web site home page, sales letter, articles, teleclasses.
- Your ezine (online magazine to stay in touch with your audience).
- Online short articles to submit to opt-in ezines and top web sites.
- Book signing/talk information.
- Radio interview questions.
- Teleclass guest appearances.
- Media kit/power press release.
- Ideal book review.
- Business cards.
- Brochures.
- Flyers.
- Final testimonials.
- All other marketing information you gather.

One other approach used by Dan Poynter, Self-Publishing Guru, is to create an 8 ½ by 11 notebook with huge rings. Use this as your file. Put all of your chapter headings, how-to's and practices into it. You can carry it with you all the time, adding material as you see fit. It even looks like a book.

In Your Business File

Consider yourself a businessperson as well as an author. No one cares about your book more than you do. Learn the business of self-publishing, such as Print-on-Demand (POD), ePublishing, and how to promote and market your book Online as well as traditional ways so you get what you deserve as an author—sales, adventure, credibility.

It's a great journey, and if you don't know how to do a particular part of the business, you can hire the appropriate professional. And you can do it on a budget! In a separate file, start adding such business files as: Epublishing, Promoting on the Internet, Developing a Web site, Printing the book, People to delegate particular tasks to, Your expenses for tax deductions later.

> **Author's Tip:** Authors who organize their material are much more able to write each chapter faster, each book faster, and get them published and sold faster.

By organizing the parts of your book either in hard files, computer files, or both, you will be able to move faster to complete your book. While some of you just want to write a print book, those who are open to eBook opportunities should read the next chapter that shares benefits, who will profit most from an eBook, and where to sell your eBook.

E-Book Opportunities

Want to write and publish an eBook? Your opportunities and benefits abound.

Ebooks are a great non-traditional way to write, publish, and market your books. The opportunities are immense if your targeted market and you are somewhat Internet savvy. People buy all kinds of books on the Web–business, romance, relationship, self-help, and novels. Like me, you can learn the game, if you are willing.

EPublishing is here to stay. Bookcoaching clients often ask, " Doesn't a print book with one of the top publishers bring you more prestige?" Well, maybe, but think of the long process (over 2 years) to get there. They only accept 1% submissions from unknown authors because they don't think they can make enough money on you.

Today more people want shorter how-to books because their reading time is limited. For fiction, they want a fast read too. Just think of your own reading habits. Wouldn't a to-the-point book serve you well? Business readers especially want information in short and easy formats and love the Internet. So, keep an open mind and think ePublishing.

What many writers don't realize is that you can write a print book and an eBook at the same time. In Chapter Two, you learned how to make two Word files of the same information. You discovered you could write the eBook shorter with fewer stories and long descriptions.

Before we talk about length and format of the different models of eBooks and what each offers you, let me remind you of the possibilities and payoffs.

Is ePublishing for you?

EPublishing is not for everyone. If you are considering ePublishing, ask yourself:

- Who am I trying to reach? (Think the #1 biggest audience—Online)
- Who are my potential readers? (They are not in the book store, but Online looking for information) -
- Will Online readers want my book as an eBook? (Yes, they want information right now and don't want to wait for snail mail.
- How comfortable am I Online? (You can get more savvy with a coach)
- Are my buyers comfortable with the Internet? (Billions are)
- What formats are my readers comfortable with? (They like short, easy-to-read eBooks)
- Am I willing to get over the short learning curve to get thousands of sales instead of hundreds? (I got mentors and coaches 4 years ago, and now my books are top sellers)
- Is my product more valuable when delivered fast? (In today's instant society, yes. Online shoppers love to download a book immediately on the Web site that sells your book.)

Author's Note: What I love about this great adventure: I...

- Sell enough books each month for over ½ my income.
- Meet other friendly and fascinating people Online who love to network.
- Get to do the whole thing from my home office—no book schlepping, no panty hose, no travel.
- Play an much easier promotion and marketing game
- Spend far less time and money (Online promotion is mostly free).
- Have more fun because I don't have to chase a black rainbow with no pot of gold at its end like traditional marketing

Benefits of ePublishing

- Makes publishing time shorter, sometimes by years.
- Gets you to market faster to produce faster cash flow.

- Creates thousands more targeted Online audiences eager to buy.

- Gives you a publishing way that is less expensive, cost-effective.

- Moves you to more profits—no mailing costs and time.

- Expands your Online markets to millions.

- Helps you update material fast and easy.

- Gives you convenience from your home office.

- Gets you cheaper digital format.

- Eliminates inventory problems and expenses like print books

These benefits are just a few. But you get the idea.

Author's Hot Selling Tip: Write how-to eBooks that solve your reader's problem or challenge. Save them time, $, create satisfying relationships, feel healthier, expand their spiritual life, find a mate, and make their lives better.

Where to Sell your Book?

The best place to sell your book is through your own Web site or through your email lists such as ezine subscribers, potential clients, or customers. To put up a five-page Web site you can get a top Web master for around $600. Some of you may not want to go that direction yet, but if you do, you'll get all the profits from your eBook and get a higher price for it too.

Check These Selling eBook Web Sites Out:

You can publish at some of these with a few restrictions, but each of these sites have rules so be sure to see the fine print before you jump.

1. BookLocker—Pays royalties and you can sell your book elsewhere. New submission guidelines online at http://www.booklocker.com/get-published.html.

2. Amazon.com—To submit an eBook on Amazon, I recommend you talk to the master who knows how to get your book on Amazon. Marshall Masters has a distributor account with them.

3. IUniverse.com—This company does it all, but the author doesn't get complete control over the book. Although it's less money to get started, you must buy your books from this company at their price.

4. 1stBooks.com—This company will do your POD and offer distribution for your print books.. Beware of the fine print so you don't lose here.

5. BarnesandNoble.com—Discounts offered to buyers. Read details on how to sell your book there.

6. Borders.com—To sell your book, this site takes you to Amazon.com.

7. Ojster.com—Reviews fiction books with link to where sold.

8. InfinityPublishing.com—Offers print on demand and Ingram as distributor. For retail sales they offer your book on their site. Author gets 20%. They distribute to wholesale for you too. While they list many books on their site, they offer promotion at a once a year conference.

Fiction Online eBook Stores

As Web sites come and go, check into these and see if they fit your needs.

1. Fictionworks.com

2. LTDbooks.com

3. ebooks.palmone.com

4. writingcareer.com/ebooks.shtml

5. bartleby.com/ebook

To define the different kinds of eBooks and what they will do or not do for you the author I turn to is my trusted colleague. Marshall Masters, President of Your Own World Books, is a 20-year publisher who gets the author way out there to the world, beyond the world I inhabited before meeting him. Besides the free article Online promotion where I do to make big sales, take a good look at this information, then decide which ways are best for you.

Tools to Help You Write That Book – Fast

Microsoft Office – 97/2000/2003/XP

A good place to look for lowest prices for all versions of MS Office and other software is: http://shopper.cnet.com.

Most everyone already has a copy of Microsoft Word of some version. If you do not, you can shop the Internet for an OEM version. These are the full install disks that usually come with a new computer and do not include printed documentation. Whichver version of Word you get, make sure you also get Microsoft PowerPoint. While PowerPoint is intended for presentations, it is a great eBook graphic creator when used in conjunction with SnagIt Screen Capture (see below.)

WordPerfect Office 12, Small Business Edition $179.00

http://www.corel.com

WordPerfect offers an excellent word processing program. Before Microsoft dominated the field, WordPerfect was the top selling word processor and still is for the legal market. What makes this office suite a real bargain is that it includes Paint Shop Pro 9. This is an author-friendly paint program for making great graphics.

OpenOffice 2.0 $FREE

http://openoffice.org

This is the open source version of Micrsoft Office. It is comprable to Office 97 and is immediately familiar to anyone who has used any MS Office product. It offers a full suite of word process, prestation graphics and spreadsheet tools. When comparing file sizes between MS Office and OpenOffice, expect the OpenOffice variant to be roughly half as big. A real help when authoring large manuscripts. Given that it is free, every writer should have get it at http:// openoffice.org.

PDF eBook Maker

If someone is going to produce eBooks for sale from their own Web site, they need a good PDF application that can give them rich editing features and security. For eBooks, you can add hyperlink buttons for improved navigation.

Adobe Acrobat 7 Professional US$449.00

http://www.adobe.com/products/acrobatpro/main.html

This is the application we use at yowbooks.com as part of creating pre-press PDF file and Adobe eBooks for distribution.

PDF Converter 3 Professional US$99.00

http://www.scansoft.com/pdfconverter/professional/features.asp#create

A superb technology company.

Add Some Graphics

SnagIt Screen Capture $39

http://www.techsmith.com/products/snagit/default.asp?lid=SnagItHome

Regardless of whether the author is using Adobe or Scansoft for PDF cre-ation, a handy universal graphics tool for every author is Snagit by Techsmith. You use the tool to capture the exact image you want. You can use it with PowerPoint to create nice ebook graphics. It is simple to use, and you get a great, simple graphic every time.

> **PDF eBook Tip:** When creating graphics for the Adobe PDF (also known as Glassbook) you want to use a setting of 150 DPI with RGB colors. This will give your books an optimal display quality on today's new flat panel screens.

Advanced JPEG Compressor $25

http://www.winsoftmagic.com/index.html

If your ebook is going to contain a lot of inline graphics, this has a direct impact on file size, download speeds and usability. The Advanced JPEG Com-pressor reduces the file size for graphics used by all the popular eBook for-mats. You can optimize your graphics for the best appearances while dramatically reducing the file size.

Publishing Ebooks On The Cheap—Three Winning Strategies

You want your eBook to sell, and you want to produce it the cheapest, fastest way. Right?

Whether you're bringing your first self-published book to market on a thin dime, or you want a cheap way to sell more print books, eBook publishing offers new opportunities for the little guys to win on the cheap.

The defining moment for eBook publishing happened in March 2000, when Stephen King offered, "Riding the Bullet," a 66-page King ghost story on Amazon.com in the Adobe eBook format. Demand was so immediate and immense, that Amazon's servers literally could not keep up for days, and King eventually sold a half-million digital copies of that e-novella without spending a single cent for typesetting, printing, warehousing, returns and all other steep costs associated with print publishing. However, what worked well for King has not worked with the same results for others, and the eBook phenomena has had some teething pains, as do all new technologies.

Are eBooks a passing fad as some pundits argue? Not if you look at the numbers. The sales of eBooks on the Internet have steadily grown since King published his electronic novella and the growth rate has been 30% per year for the last two years. This makes eBooks one of the fastest growing sectors of the publishing industry today.

For savvy self-publishers, there are three basic opportunity strategies:

- Publishing on the Cheap with eDocs and eBooks
- Selling More Print Books with DRM-format eBooks
- Riding the Crest of the Electronic Publishing Wave to Big Profits

Strategy #1 – Publishing on the Cheap with eDocs and eBooks

Most PC users are familiar with the term "eBooks" but sometimes the term "eDoc" comes drifting by. Knowing the difference is vital to publishing on the cheap.

- EDOC: This term predates "eBook" and refers to any digital document produced primarily for use as a print file. Web sites, authors, and businesses write eDocs calling them eBooks. So, there is a common use version, but in the technical world, these eBooks are called eDocuments.

  EDocs are the best way to distribute for highly formatted electronic documents for local printing, such as like technical guides and brochures. Everyone has been using office programs such as word processors and presentation managers to create eDocs for decades. If you want to create your eDoc to be printed by your buyers, you will keep the pages around

100 pages, and probably use the 8½ by 11" format to be read by Adobe Readers. Expect a minimal learning curve here if you're an experienced PC user. However, eBooks can be a different thing.

- EBOOK: While an eBook can be printed (if the author permits), the primary use is for on-screen reading. While an eDoc is formatted for printing to Letter or A4 office paper, an eBook is formatted for easy on-screen reading. A true eBook will be about 1/3 of a page in size and the formatting and typesetting will use a simple design for optimum onscreen readability. For a good example of formatted ebooks, check the free Yowbooks.com demos <yowbooks.com/html/demos.html> and see the difference for yourself.

If you want to publish your own eBook or eDoc there is only one format to consider: the Adobe Acrobat PDF format (also referred to as Glassbook.) This is the same format Stephen King used with "Riding the Bullet, and he sold half a million copies. A big reason for King's success is that more computers are installed with the Adobe Reader than any other eBook or eDoc reader program out there.

To create great Portable Document Format (PDF) eBooks and eDocs, you'll need a PDF program that gives you the ability to set security permissions for content copying, printing, and file modification.

Publishing pros use Adobe Acrobat Professional but if you get a jolt of stick shock when you see the price, there are alternatives like Docudek's deskPDF Professional program <www.docudesk.com> for a fraction of the cost.

Or, you can hire the Portable Document Format (PDF) service from a professional coach or consultant.

If you want a great eDoc and eBook-authoring tool for free, check out Open Office <openoffice.org>. The latest versions look and work much like MS Office. The big difference is that is more stable than MS Office and runs on Widows, Mac, and Linux PCs. Use Open Office to author a slick book and use Adobe or Docudek to add security and other PDF format features.

Hot-Selling Tip for PDF

As you see in this book you can also put in Web sites and emails in hyperlinks so that, if the person is connected to the Internet, they can click right from the book through to any Web page you want them to see. You can also put sound, pictures, and video in the PDF file.

When your eBook or eDoc is ready to go, the top choice is to sell it from your own Web site. Some authors offer a download link for the PDF eBooks and eDocs they sell. That is convenient delivery method, but limited in terms of controlling possible piracy and illegal copying.

> **Author's Tip:** If you're selling expensive digital content, deliver it via E-mail. Be sure to include a copyright notice in the body of the E-mail in big letters. An example notice is:

> The scanning, uploading and distribution of this book via the Internet or via any other means without the permission of the publisher is illegal and punishable by law. Please purchase only authorized electronic editions, and do not participate in or encourage the electronic piracy of copyrighted materials. Please support the author's rights.

When your E-mail shows up with an eBook attached and a strong notice, you remind the customer subtly reminded of two things. You enforce your copy-rights and by sending your book to their E-mail account and you've created an evidence trail that leads to them.

Want to Sell More Books?

Most potential buyers will not make a local call to buy. They also prefer to buy with a credit card. You need to install these tools before big profits come. Here's some ideas.

One. Open a PayPal merchant account. It is free and if you honor legitimate refund requests, and works quite well. Judy and I use this service.

Three drawbacks.

1. PayPal is a little pricey in terms of merchant transaction fees–Seven %

2. Some USA customers hate PayPal. You'll lose them if you do not offer payment by money order, cashier check, or other service such as MTC Business (see below).

3. PayPal is difficult to use for International customers. It can take up to 30 days for foreign buyers to setup a PayPal account.

Two. Contact www.ClickBank.com for service at your site where your cus-tomer can download your book immediately. Ask you Web master to set this up for you. Also a 7% charge. Judy uses this service.

Three. Contact MTC Business Support Services at 1800-366-5596 or go to their Web site www.mtcbiz.net, or email mtcbiz@pacbell.net

Any of Judy's readers or clients get a $25 discount when they mention her name. MTC also charges a 7% fee until you sell so much, you'll add a change of service. Judy says that it's the best money she's spent because their service is so good. A real person at a real phone number for your buyers who prefer the phone. When you get the order, you call Tony's toll-free number with your order. Then you send the eBook from your home office and record your credit information by phone to keep it secure. Over 80% of Judy's sales come this way. Remember, many women and non-techies prefer to order by phone. Always give your customer several easy ways to buy from you.

Hot Selling Point: When you get to the point where your monthly sales are $1,000 or more, you need to do two things. First, start shopping for your own Bankcard Merchant account so you can accept credit cards directly (but continue to offer PayPal or Clickbank as an option.) Then, set aside a month's profits and go play with the big boys by distributing your next eBook globally as a DRM-formatted eBook. Now the fun starts!

Strategy #2 – Selling More Print Books with DRM-format eBooks

You can sell a eBooks from your own Web site, but if you want to sell a lot more books, you need distribution with major booksellers like www.Amazon.com and www.Powells.com. These heavy hitters use the Big "4" formats: Adobe, Microsoft, Mobipocket and Palm.

All Big "4" formats share the following characteristics:

Major Bookseller Support: There are many excellent eBook formats, with loads of great features. However the Big "4" are the ones supported by the big global Online eBook resellers. Always start with one or more of the Big "4" and go from there.

If you have several inexpensive fiction titles in your catalog and want to distribute with the Big "4" formats plus 4 other less known formats, try submitting your title to the Fictionwise.com site. If they offer you a distribution contract, take it. They do a brilliant job of non-encrypted multi-format eBook sales and have a very large eBook buying audience.

Proprietary Formats: The eBook files of proprietary formats require eBook reader applications from the same software company. Adobe uses the PDF format, LIT for Microsoft, PRC for Mobipocket and PDB for Palm. In other words, a Palm eBook reader cannot use Microsoft LIT files and so forth.

This means you need to check the installed base for the format. Adobe and Microsoft are primarily used on desktop PCs and are great for big books. Mobipocket and Palm are primarily used on PDA's and handheld readers. Novella length books (20,000 to 30,000 words, which equate to Judy: ???? pages work best with these formats.

Digital Rights Management (DRM): In simple terms, DRM lets publishers and distributors control how eBooks are used by the end user. From the publishing point of view, DRM is about preventing the theft and illegal pirating of your content. When you sell a book through Amazon, it is locked to the reader installed in the customer's computer. You can copy it as you like, but it is unusable anywhere else.

If you have several fiction and nonfiction titles in your catalog and need DRM distribution, start with Mobipocket.com when seeking a distribution account. If you strike out, consider an eBook aggregator.

Using an eBook Aggregator: An aggregator will hold one or more distribution channel accounts and can place your titles into the global market. You will retain your copyright, but your eBooks must be released to market with the aggregator's imprint and ISBN numbers. For more information about eBook aggregation, visit the Your Own World Books web site <www.yowbooks.com>.

Why do eBook distributors prefer aggregators to self-publishers? Distributing multi-format eBooks demands a heavy investment of time, expertise and money, because of dissimilar reader formats and distribution methods in use today. Consequently, distributors do not have the time to support a lot of little accounts struggling with their learning curve issues.

For most authors it boils down to this. Most authors can write an entire book in the time it takes them to learn how to publish and distribute multi-format eBooks. Where is your time best spent?

Strategy Three. Riding the Crest of the Electronic Publishing Wave to Big Profits

When you hear the stock market gurus brag about how much their clients earn they always say the same thing. "If you're serious about making money, I'll show you how to get in on the bottom and out at the top." While this certainly is a crystal ball view of the world, those who invest with the Warren Buffets of the world do rather nicely.

If one applies Warren Buffet logic to the publishing industry, a clear picture forms immediately – eBooks will eventually displace print books

"Just how on Earth could eBooks ever displace print books," some might cry out. (And by the way, what does "displacement" mean?) Let's answer that with something other than a crystal ball.

Do you still have a phonograph turntable hooked up to your home stereo? If you're an audiophile who only settles for the optimum experience you most likely do, and it no doubt cost you a small fortune. However, if you're like the vast majority of us, you use an inexpensive CD or MP3 player, because you gave your old phonograph player to Goodwill years ago. A similar thing is now happening with publishing and the harbingers are already in here. Just read the headlines in your newspaper.

"Current Market Fears of $100/barrel Oil Prices " headline is not only sending shivers through Wall Street—publishers are worried too. This is because today's print publishing today is a dead weight cost industry, born of cheap energy. Consequently, it is just as vulnerable to soaring energy costs as air-lines.

Given that China has become an oil-thirsty economic juggernaut competing for already strained resources, the print publishing industry faces a troubled future indeed. Ergo, eBooks will become a saving grace for print publishers who are already situated between the looming rock of higher energy prices and the hard place of consumer resistance to higher retail prices. Libraries are big on eBooks today also.

Industries are like water. They take the path of least resistance and that is why large publishers are already putting the mechanisms in place for a shift. The old ISBN catalog system was developed for print books and has not proven adaptable to the new demands of electronic publishing. For this reason, large publishers have pushed a new catalog system that uses something called a Digital Object Identifier (DOI) into being to meet this future need. (You can see a live DOI at DOIeasylink.NET.)

On a parallel track, hardware manufacturers are ramping up for the coming demand for eBooks, and the tip of this spear is Sony. Last year they intro-duced a new handheld reader in the Japan market only. Roughly the size of a trade paperback and the first of its kind, this high-resolution reader is as easily on the eyes as the morning paper that hits your doorstep each day. Once it hits

America's shores, the price will be under $100 and these slim handheld readers will be able to store and display hundreds of your favorite books using a few inexpensive AAA batteries.

Considering that the typical eBook sells for about half of what we pay for print books, the economic case will be immediate. Sure, we'll always want more expensive print books, but just not that many of them.

Unquestionably, this is creating some short-term chaos for print publishers, but the big boys have seen it coming from a long way off, and they're dealing with it rather nicely thank you. However, for self-publishing authors this is a rare, succulent moment, because as the old saying goes, "In chaos is opportunity." Or more to the point, how do self-publishers and small presses get in on the bottom – right alongside the big guys.

Simple. Publish your new titles in all of the Big "4" eBook formats: Adobe, Microsoft, Mobipocket and Palm. Not just one or maybe two. Do all 4, because when that better mousetrap of a handheld eBook reader appears there will be a Kentucky Derby-style scramble for the lead.

- **Adobe:** Favored to win by most, the format sucks up storage and processing power like a Hoover upright. A strong runner to win, but not a sure bet by any means. Bet to place.

- **Microsoft:** They'd rather eat their young than support another operating system. Bet to place. Never to win.

- **Mobipocket:** Their reader work on everything from PCs to cell phones. Expect brilliance from this small French software company. Bet on them to show unless they suddenly find a sugar daddy with deep pockets.

- **Palm:** The dark horse with real legs. The current Palm format is a relic compared to the others, but Palm is the only handheld hardware manufacturer. If they decide to go toe-to-toe with Sony, they'll run a new young steed with great legs. Safe to place, and a great long shot bet to win.

What happens if none of the Big "4" even cross the finish line. No worries. This game is going to be about installed customer bases and if an unknown shows up out of nowhere, it will be able to read at least one, if not all four the Big "4" eBook formats. No matter who comes in first, you're winner every time.

If you are technologically inclined, and intend to write multiple books, you can buy the whole package from Adobe.

Author's Note: Choose any of the eBook Formats above, it's up to you, the author.

Compare benefits and prices to get your book into any of these formats. Depending on the deal you want, go forward and get self-published with professional help.

If you don't have a Web site and want one for you book, be sure to read my eBook (eDocument to print) *How to Create your Web Pages with Marketing Pizzazz* on my Web site, www.bookcoaching.com. This title will be changed to *Power Writing for Web Sites That Sell* and offered in all the formats above including print. I always offer the updated version free. This is the book to read before you call your Webmaster.

Who knows? With as fast as technology improves, more choices will be available tomorrow.

Author's Book Hot Selling Points—Getting your Ducks in a Row

Point One. Market you eBook on the Internet when you get close to completion. You may be sold on the traditional path, but open your mind to a much easier, faster and cheaper way to get your book into thousands of your readers hands.

You'll get targeted free traffic to the Web site where you sell your book, you'll get thousands of daily visitors on your own Web site, and you'll do it all from your home office. Writing and submitting short articles to opt-in or subscribe to ezines to your topic is the number one way to promote Online. People who subscribe and Web masters all over the world want your information.

Your payoff? They see your sales-oriented signature file and will flock to your Web site for more. When they see your articles or excerpts on top Web sites with much higher traffic than most in your subject, their visitors will come to where your book and its sales letter is posted. Like your author, your search engine status will multiply exponentially. Listed on 16,000 other sites, these numbers grow 1000 each month with this book promotion.

The more ezines and sites you submit your articles and tips to, the more people will visit your Web site or book-selling site, selling far more books than you dreamed of! Find out how in my book, *Ten Non Techie Ways to Market your Book Online.*

Point Two. Review your Web site and ask yourself does it include these Four Essentials?

1. One or two best testimonials that link to your book's sales letter.

2. Your book's sales letter to include the essential ten parts plus order page.

3. Benefit-Driven headlines on the home page that sizzle to get your visitor to buy.

4. Other enticements to get your visitor to stay a while and revisit often. Articles, useful content such as resources, and your own eNewsletter (ezine).

Once you have your excellent eBook, your ePromotion, and sizzling Web site ready, your book sales will amaze you. In the next chapter, discover how to choose your book's best format for your publishing and promotion purposes. Know you can write an eBook and print book at the same time. See Judy's "Four Format Options" to compare money saving ideas.

How to Choose Your Book's Format

Do You Want to Write a Short Book, a Print Book, or an eBook?

Maybe you want to apply all three of these formats.

Benefits of a short book: They sell well because busy people want to skim for specific solutions to their challenges.

Benefits of a print book: Some people will always want to touch the pages, so print about 200 units for your back of the room audience.

Benefits of an eBook, also known as an eDocument: Business people and others love eBooks and are willing to print them up to one hundred pages. People like instant download delivery, and they want short pieces to read, one a time. They can even choose not to print the whole book. Most of us don't read the whole book, anyway.

Your Book's Length

You don't have to write a 200-page book to be a respected author. Remember *The One-Minute Manager* and *The One-Minute Sales Person?* They are around one hundred pages each, selling millions of copies. Pulitzer Prize winner, Anna Quindlen's *A Short Guide to a Happy Life* is a hardback best seller at 2343 words, the size of a chapter or two.

Today's nonfiction book-buying audience has changed. Their biggest complaint is, "I don't have enough time." They want their information in a concise form that is easy to read and understand. If they need or want your information, they will appreciate it in any short format: special reports, workbooks, guides or eBooks of thirty to one hundred pages.

Write Your Book to Fit Your Purpose

While shorter formats may not always be accepted in bookstores or libraries, they are hot sellers at the back-of-the-room seminar and conference sales and on the Internet. When we know that we don't have to sell in bookstores and libraries, that liberates us to try more non-traditional paths.

> **Author's Note:** Tree Books are printed books; eBooks are electronically produced. Most authors hire someone to put their book into Portable Document Format (PDF). Or find a program Online to use.

> **Remember...** You can write your eBook and your print book at the same time.

Short Books are a Good Start

To reach the audience who likes information short and sweet, consider a booklet (six to fifty pages), a special report (three to fifteen pages), a workbook (seven to thirty pages), a print book of seventy-five pages or more, or an ebook of around thirty to eighty pages. These numbers are approximates, but the idea is that you have choice.

It's a good idea to start small and to put your first effort into an eBook. This can get your writing bones gathered and make the task easier and faster. Change to a longer format if it seems right. You are an individual! You're unique! You have many messages and plenty of material, but they don't all have to be in one book. One big mistake that emerging authors make is that they want to write an end-all, be-all book, and they write for a general audience rather than a specific one.

Think of your life, your business and how much time you want to dedicate to a book. Be realistic! If you already work thirty to forty hours a week, to stay balanced and healthy, you'll only want to spend ten to twenty hours a week on one writing project. Write one that you can finish in about a month, so you don't lose heart and don't finish.

Booklets / Guides / Manuals / Workbooks can be ten to fifty pages. If printed, you can staple them or use a coil binder. For myself, I keep them simple and just stapled at the copy shop to keep prices down. I put my forty to ninety- page books into a heavy plastic sleeve that I get at Office Depot. They can be any size from 8 ½" by 11" down to 6" by 9".

Paulette Ensign created her best-selling booklet *110 Ideas for Organizing Your Business Life* numbering the ideas in eight pages. It fits in a business envelope, making it easy to mail. Individually, it's $5, but Paulette's biggest profits are in group sales and consulting. It depends on your book's purpose. Visit her Web site www.tipsbooklets.com.

Through my publishing company, Skills Unlimited, I wrote and sold 20 self-help and health booklets and special reports in the 8 ½" by 11" workbook format, selling hundreds of thousands over the years. The *Ten Ways to Super-memory, Conquering Clutter and Procrastination* and *Beyond Speedreading* manuals are still great sellers.

Special Reports contain specific information and skills targeted to a business audience. They can be as short as a few pages to as long as fifteen or so. They sell for $3.95 to $35.95 depending on the pages and information. You can turn some longer articles into special eReports to give away. Mention only one in your signature file at the bottom of each email you send out. These reports help market your longer books as well as offer a potential client or customer a piece of you at low-cost. It's good to offer products in several price categories to meet your audience's needs.

> **Author's Tip:** You don't even have to author all the reports yourself! Team up with other authors in your field. Include a cassette or CD-ROM. Bundle several booklets or special reports together to sell at the back of the room. One speaker I know made $500 sales each time she spoke, and she didn't write a single book.

> **Author's Smile:** Have you read the shortest book written? *What Men Know About Women?* When you open it, all the pages are blank! It sold 750,000 copies.

Workbooks are usually 8 ½ by 11". They contain some information and some exercises to do within their covers. Useful at seminars, they also sell well at the back of the room.

If you want to sell your workbook as an eBook I recommend you add some chapter formatting, too, such as that in Chapter Seven of this book. Give your reader examples of what your want them to do. Don't just put a question up with blank spaces. Your reader needs help getting started.

> **Author's Tip:** Short books take less time, attract a bigger audience, get published faster and yield higher profits.

Your Book's Size

What is your book's purpose? Did you write it to teach a skill, inform, solve a problem, tell a unique story, be a useful resource, or be a forum where your audience can respond, such as a workbook?

For your workbook, special report, manual or booklet of 5 ½ by 7 or 8 ½ by 11 inches, you can have it either saddle stitched (stapled inside), comb bound (with rings), in a plastic sleeve, stapled in the upper left hand corner, or with two or three staples on the left side. Check out your printers and copy shops to see the variety of possibilities.

A Perfect-Bound Book

A perfect-bound book, whether soft or hard cover, will have a well-designed, four-color cover and a spine that has your book title and publishers' logo on it. It looks like the other trade books on your bookstore or library shelves. It is usually 5 ½" by 8 ½" or 6 by 9 inches. Using POD technology, you can produce your book to look like other traditional ones.

> **Author's Note:** You may want to change your mind about comb bound books. They end up costing as much, if not more than a perfect-bound book.

Your book's format is a personal decision. Think about your audience, your market place, and how you will sell it. You can even write a book in more than one format. First, write an eBook, then a special report, and then a compilation of articles or stories that become a longer eBook or print book.

Final Words

You have a good start on the way to multiple books and sales. Following the strategies in this book will make the path so much easier. If you want more help, please see my Web site at www.bookcoaching.com. If you need one-on-one bookcoaching, just email me at Judy@bookcoaching.com or call my toll-free number 888/200-9743.

Would you like to subscribe to my free monthly ezine "The Book Coach Says...??" Dan Poynter, author of *The Self-Publishing Manual*, says, "It's chocked full of useful information and worth your time." Just visit my Web site at www.bookcoaching.com or www.bookcoaching.com/opt-in.shtml.

Bonus Report #1

Promoting Books @ The Speed of Thought

by Dan Poynter

Publishing is changing—for the better. There is a New Model for book writing, producing, selling and promoting. One part of this revolutionary change is in book promoting.

Here are several ways to use new technology to promote your book faster, easier and cheaper.

Broadcast email, done properly, is not spam. Book announcements should only be sent to existing customers, potential customers on opt-in lists and targeted members of the press. Most of these people are in your personal address book. Match your offer to those who have already expressed an interest in this type of information.

Make your publishing company Web-site centric. Put your book and all your basic promotion documents on your site and print from the site when you need hard copies. Don't maintain a stock of dealer bulletins and news releases in your office. Keep the masters in your cyber pressroom and retrieve them when required. For an example of a pressroom, see http://parapub.com/getpage.cfm?file=pressroom/pressroom.html

If you speak on the subject of your book, set up a speaking sub-site with all the information on what you can do. Post your speech descriptions, client list, fee schedule, facilities forms, speaking calendar, audio/video clips, etc. Replace your press kits; avoid printing and mailing. For an example of a speaking sub-site, see http://parapub.com/getpage.cfm?file=/speaking/index.html

Help the information-seeking potential customer to make a buying decision. Give enough information on the book. Provide the same shopping experience they have in a store. If you are publishing fiction, put the first chapter on your site as a free read. The first chapter in a creative work will give the reader a taste and is designed to keep the buyer reading. If your work is nonfiction, provide the first page or so of each chapter to give the browser an idea of what is in the book. If you need help setting up your web site on this model, contact Mary Westheimer at http://www.BookZone.com. BookZone hosts the web-sites for some 3,500 book publishers.

For the media, put the entire book in a unique address section (URL) along with your promotional materials. Email a pitch letter to the editors and reviewers and invite them to your web site to see your book, and media kit: bio, testimonials, news releases, etc. Tell them what is in the "media kit" and remind them they will save time because they do not have to retype the material. Let them read the book free online. Capture the reviewer's address when they log on. Add the reviewer to your list and notify them directly when you are promoting your next book. The mission is to design an online media kit that is so useful, the reviewers will flock to use it. And, self-service will save you a lot of time and money.

Publishers Weekly and USA Today recently reviewed their first eGalleys. Invite reviewers to your site and offer to send an eGalley. Promotion @ the speed of email is the wave of the future.

Do the reviewers want eGalleys? PW, for example, receives over 100 galleys each day. They select a handful and the rest go to a holding room. Periodically, someone comes to clean out the room. EGalleys avoid this solid-waste disposal challenge.

Subsidiary rights. Send an email to editors of newsletters, magazines and ezines and offer them the opportunity to excerpt parts of your book free. Ask them to include source, copyright and ordering information at the end of the excerpt.

To find the email addresses for magazines and newsletters, see http://parapub. com/getpage.cfm?file=/bookprom.html and http://www.opinion-pages.org

Email promotions can result in slightly fewer responses than traditional mailings and follow-up telephone calls. But the costs in time and money are far less and the responses begin immediately.

Foreign Rights. Use email to ask foreign publishers if they would like to buy subsidiary rights and translate your book into their language. Send publishers directly to a rights section on your Web site. That section will provide a complete book, author bio, testimonials, cover image, news releases, back cover sales copy and other promotional materials. Capture their address when they log on. Then follow up with email.

For foreign publisher email addresses, see International Literary Market Place. It lists publishers outside North America by country. Start with the major language groups: Germany, France, Italy, Spain and Japan. Select publishers that publish in your subject area. If you can't find many, email the national publishing association for that particular country, describe your book and ask for suggested matching publishers.

See the RightsCenter at http://www.rightscenter.com and PMA's Foreign Rights Virtual Book Fair at http://pma-online.org/pmafair/index.cfm.

Use every means possible to send people to your site. List your URL in ads, your .sig, and anywhere you might ordinarily leave your telephone number.

Replace expensive four-color brochures with less expensive business cards. Your card should have a photograph of the book's cover, your usual contact information and a list of all the resources that can be found on your Web site. Use the cards to drive traffic to your web site. For great prices on cards, see http://www.MWMdexter.com

Related Web Sites. Surf the Web for sites related to the subject of your book. When you find one that matches, contact the owner and suggest a dealership. Get as many outlets as possible to sell your book.

Newsgroups. Take part in newsgroups related to your book's subject. Answer questions and become known as an expert on your subject. For a list of newsgroups, see Groups at http://www.excite.com, http://www.YahooGroups.com and http://www.deja.com.

Promotion services. Do not hire the spammers who flood your email box with offers to promote your site or product. Doing so will cost you a lot of money, incur the wrath of potential customers and will encourage more spam.

Direct Contact Media Services will send out your news release to carefully selected media via fax and email. Paul Krupin will rewrite your news release to make it more useful to the media. He will send the announcement to 1,500 to 2,500 targeted print, radio and TV outlets. 1500 one-page releases cost $300. Contact him at dircon@owt.com and see http://www.book-publicity.com.

For more ideas on promoting books online, see U-Publish.com by Dan Poynter and Danny O. Snow. See http://www.u-publish.com.

New computer programs, new printing processes and the Web are transforming the writing, producing, disseminating and promoting of information. Books will never be the same. The winners are author, publishers and readers.

In the future, nonfiction book publishing will see minimized inventories and maximized relationships between authors and customers (readers). Publishing will become customer-centric and "books" will thrive on uniqueness, customization and variety. Book writing, publishing, selling and promoting are changing—for the better.

Writing periodicals

Dan Poynter does not want you to die with a book still inside you. You have the ingredients and he has your recipe. Dan has written more than 100 books since 1969 including Writing Nonfiction and The Self-Publishing Manual. For more help on book writing, see http://ParaPub.com. © 2003

or

Book Publishing periodicals

Dan Poynter, the Voice of Self-Publishing, has written more than 100 books since 1969 including Writing Nonfiction and The Self-Publishing Manual. Dan is a past vice-president of the Publishers Marketing Association. For more help on book publishing and promoting, see http://ParaPub.com. © 2003

or

Professional Speaking periodicals

Dan Poynter has written more than 100 books since 1969 including Writing Nonfiction and The Self-Publishing Manual. He is past-chair of NSA's Writer-Publisher PEG and the founder of the PEG newsletter. For more help on book writing, publishing and promoting, see http://ParaPublishing.com. © 2003

Bonus Report #2

Print on Demand (POD) Publishers – the Good, the Bad, and the Ugly

Marshall Masters

The costs of self-publishing a book have fallen by 75% or more, thanks to Print on demand (POD) publishing. This new print technology, based on the common office copier, has opened with a broad range of new opportunities for self-publishing authors with limited budgets. Regrettably, it has also created new opportunities for those seeking to exploit first time authors. This article shows you how to win while avoiding the pitfalls. First, we'll look at POD publishers – the good, the bad and the ugly. Then we'll look at three handy POD profit tips that will steer you toward what works, and away from what hurts.

The Good

The good POD publisher wants a win-win deal – the book that makes a profit for everyone involved. Up front costs are the highest, but you'll get personal attention, a great book and a great deal on the back end where the real money is made. As with all POD publishers, you will retain your copyright and you will be able to set a realistic market price for your work with full access to global print and electronic bookseller distribution channels.

There are many good POD publishers doing business today. They're honest, ethical companies who pride themselves in offering great value and service. Who does business with them? Successful business people who need to publish a book to brand their business and self-publishing authors who were shortchanged by their last publisher.

How do you spot a good POD publisher? Seasoned self-publishers go straight to the back end of the deal. They're looking for what really counts: Maximum value, control, and profits, plus professionals who take a personal interest. You'll pay more on the front end, but a good POD publisher always keeps your best interests at heart. Like the old saying goes, "you get what you pay for." These POD businesses only work with authors who will spend time and money on promotion.

The Bad

The bad POD publisher wants a win-lose deal. No matter how much you lose, they always win. This is not to say they are bad people, because they're not. They are simply good business people offering a bad deal if you happen to be a motivated self-publisher. Forget the glowing testimonials. To the contrary, their businesses are structured around writers who don't read the fine print and don't question the high price and no promotion of their book. They think the upfront low cost is a real deal. These publishers offer a loss leader price on the front-end to get the business; then take heavy profits on the overpriced books the author invariably peddles to friends and family because he fears self-promotion.

Now here is the shocker. Bad POD publishers land about 70% of the first-time author deals out there, so spotting them is easy. They'll invariably brag about the hundreds or thousands of titles in their catalogs. However, ask their sales representatives how many of their authors earned enough in royalties to recoup their publishing costs and see what happens to the brags. If your inquiry gets a creative moonwalking reply – there it is.

Then again, bad POD publishers do happen to be a good fit for the vast majority of first time authors. This is because most new authors won't promote their book much, and view failure as an acceptable option, consciously or not, for their book.

Ergo, if low sales work for you, choose a bad POD publisher. Join the crowd after doing one more little test. You need to search for victims, because a bad POD publisher can turn out to be a thinly veiled ugly POD publisher.

The Ugly

The ugly POD publisher offer the promise of a self-publishing "El Dorado" and preys on naïve self-publishing authors who believe that they'll beat the odds and land that coveted "standard rich and famous contract" with a minimum of effort. Like W. C. Fields said, "There's a sucker born every minute," and ugly POD publishers use this like a war chant.

At first glance, they will not be obvious. Like the bad POD publisher deal, you'll see a front-end price guaranteed to make you feel clever. However, once your book and money is committed, things will slowly turn ugly. You'll no longer be that detached shopper in total control of the deal. You'll be financially and emotionally committed author and easily stampeded because you do not understand the business. When does the stamped phase begin? When you find yourself talking to someone with the scruples of a time-share salesman. Not someone who loves books.

Sorting out ugly POD publishers takes a little work. Set aside some time and use search engines, newsgroups, or blogs to find other authors who've done business with the same publisher. If they are vocal victims, you'll find them. Send them a note and they'll pour their hearts out to you. After that, it's your call. Or in other words, why are you doing this in the first place?

POD Publishing for Love or Money

People write books for many different reasons. Some for love, some for money and others for both. If you're self-publishing your book for money, find a good POD publisher and shop for value.

If you cannot afford a good POD publisher, write a good book and sell it from your own Web site until you can sell it to a traditional publisher or have accumulated the profits to find a good POD publisher.

Before you do, spend a few coins to learn what hurts and what works from an honest bookcoach, an author's advocate who will send clients to the right choices for them. This author's two most favorite coaches are Judy Cullins <bookcoaching.com> and Dan Poynter <parapublishing.com>. Buy their books, and if they happen to be offering a low-priced teleclass, a conference call, where anyone all over the world can attend, dig down to the lint in the seam of your pocket if need be, and sign up.

After you write your book, write ad copy and build your own Web site. To write your home page and sales letter so you sell more books, contact a bookcoach who knows Web marketing. You can find inexpensive domain names and hosting services at <yowbooks.net>, as well as many other reputable service providers on the web. After that, open a PayPal merchant account. It costs nothing and when you sell books this way, the cash pops into your account like a stuck slot machine.

Talking about slot machines, let's move on those who are publishing their first book for love – and not money. In this case, let's think of POD publishing like the casinos that dot the Las Vegas landscape. Oodles of slot machines dominate the main floors of these opulent pleasure palaces. While everyone knows their dollar slots generally pay better than the nickel slots, how often do we see folks playing the dollar slots?

Rather, you see folks gambling on the rows of nickel and dime slots next to the front door and losing – but having fun too. The same holds true with self-publishing for love. If financial failure is OK, then it makes absolutely no sense to play the dollar slots. Pick the best bad POD publisher deal you can find, and play the nickel slots for fun. No matter which machine you play, the result will be that same, so just have fun. When it comes time to go home, don't spoil the glow with complaints about your empty purse, because you'll have gotten what you bargained for.

And what about first time authors who self-publish for both love and money (like moi)? Find a good coach; plan the work; and then work the plan. Find the money to do it right. Shop for value. Spend wisely and only when you must. Above all else: failure is never an option! Make that last one a 6-foot long banner and nail it in the wall over your PC.

Once you commit yourself to success, use the following three POD profit tips to squeeze every penny of profit out your self-published POD book:

- Set a Market-based Retail Price
- Control the Costs on Books You Sell
- Use 24/7 Internet Promotion to Boost Sales

POD Profit Tip #1 — Set a Market-based Retail Price

While POD publishing has slashed the entry cost of self-publishing, a nagging problem has been the absence of market-based retail POD book prices. A market-based retail price is one perceived as reasonable by consumers, and major publishers who print their books in large volumes and shape these market perceptions.

Bad and ugly POD publishers saddle their authors' books with sky-high retail prices that scare casual buyers away. Sure, they'll offer clever pricing schemes, but the final numbers will always tell the same sad story. Guaranteed profits for everyone except the author!

Avoid these 'programmed-for-failure' book-pricing schemes. Look for a good POD publisher who'll work with you to set a realistic, market-driven retail price for your book. This will put you on a level playing field with the big New York publishers who control consumer price expectations.

POD Profit Tip #2 — Control the Costs on Books You Sell

Over half of all books are sold everywhere else in America except bookstores. However, the real rub comes when it is time for the author to be paid. Royalty payments for books sold through traditional distribution methods resemble the geological ground speed of the continental drift; expect a 90-180 day lag as a rule. The big guys make the rules here, so like it or lump it, they're not about to change.

On the other hand, books you sell through your own direct efforts put immediate cash in your pocket. Consequently, you recoup your up-front investment quickly and can spend more for promotion when you need it most. That being said, the sad truth is that this is exactly where the bad and ugly POD publishers are going to cut you off at the knees.

There is an old retail axiom, "It is not what you sell it for, but what you pay for it that determines your profit." Bad and ugly POD publishers know this axiom all too well, which is why you'll never learn their actual wholesale printing costs. If you did, you'd see your sorely needed investment recovery and marketing monies going into the POD publisher's pockets, simply because you let them beat you like a drum on the front end.

If you book is a business, find a good POD publisher who'll sell you your own books for what distributors pay for them or less. Better yet, find a good POD publisher who'll publish your book and then let you negotiate directly with a printer of your own choose for rock bottom prices on the books you'll sell through your own direct marketing efforts.

POD Profit Tip #3 — Use 24/7 Internet Promotion to Boost Sales

Many bad and ugly POD publishers offer scaled-down, low-tech promotion methods designed for traditional publishers, so know this; traditional publishers only make money on 3 of every 10 books they sell. That doesn't stop them from selling you four-color business cards and bookmarkers (at a hefty markup.) While these are handy low-tech printed promotion tools, how many books will they sell while you are asleep?

For about the same cost as printed matter, you can use 24/7, low-cost Internet marketing tools such as Digital Object Identifiers (DOI) from DOIeasylink.NET, plus Google Adword and Yahoo Overture pay-per-click campaigns.

You can also use other no and low-cost, non-techie ways to market your book Online.

They include writing short articles and submitting them to subscribers of opt-in ezines in all kinds of categories. Think health, personal growth, spiritual, business, book publishing and many more. These viral marketing ways are your 24/7 sales team, always connecting book buyers with you.

Scared by the technology? Ask yourself this question. Is it better to throw your limited promotion money into an office supply cabinet, or into low-cost Internet promotion tools and techniques that drive customers to your product page on Amazon or your own Web site?

If you can find a POD publisher who'll support you with these low cost services, you'll get a much bigger bang for your promotion bucks, for about what it costs to fill an office supply cabinet with printed matter. If your POD publisher does not offer it, invest the time to learn how to do it yourself. Then do it!

Now is the Time for New Authors to Self-publish!

Everyone has to start somewhere. If this is your first book and your sole motivation is to make money, then write a how-to that offers immediate solutions to a common life crisis, such as a divorce or a tax audit.

On the other hand, what if you're not interested in how to cope with an ugly divorce or how to finesse a brutal tax audit because your passion is to write a book titled *99 Ways to Parboil an Onion*? You follow your passion of course!

There are six billion souls on the planet, and more coming each day. On top of this, the growth of the Internet is the most remarkable intellectual human event since Gutenberg invented the press. Forget the naysayer types who still haven't figured out how to set the clocks on their VCRs. The Internet is a powerful, new promotion tool for first-time self-publishing authors; especially for those with limited funds.

Be persistent and you'll find enough people on the Internet who share your love of parboiled onions and you will turn a tasty profit. Then write a cry as you peel divorce book and make a real killing.

The future has never been brighter for fully committed self-publishing writers who want their first love – writing – to be their day job for life. Yes, you can do it. Believe it.

Marshall Masters *** Author, Publisher, Speaker ***

Your Own World Books: *Your Friend in the Publishing Business*
POD and eBook publishing with Internet web presence.

Authors: Make more on every book sold.

http://dx.doi.org/10.1572/yowbooks
getpublished@yowbooks.com
http://yowbooks.com

Toll Free (877) 251-7761
Tel/Fax 775-546-1472

Bonus Report #3

How to Get Testimonials from the Rich and Famous

Judy Cullins
www.bookcoaching.com

Authors want buyers! Buyers want a sure bet your book will solve their challenges. More than any other copy, testimonials sell books. When people see testimonials from names they recognize and trust, they accept your book. The "lookie-loos" become buyers!

Why Testimonials are Number One in Selling your Book or Service

Even if your book or service is excellent, it won't sell well unless you give your potential customers a reason to buy. From the book *Write your eBook or Other Short Book—Fast! Testimonials,* you know that the back cover where you place testimonials is the number two "Essential Hot-Selling-Point. They work harder than other promotional words, so be sure to start collecting them early.

Back Cover Testimonials

Here, you will need three testimonials: one from a celebrity or leader in your field, and the others the man or woman on the street; thrilled readers. These testimonials are the most important thing to include on your back cover; better than benefits, better than your bio, because your prospective buyers trust your book more when others recommend it.

Collect many more testimonials each time you email or meet someone interested in your topic. Put these in your front pages of your book.

Web and email Sales Letters Testimonials

Sprinkle your testimonials throughout your Web site and email sales letter. If you don't have a website, ask a good book and marketing coach how to sell via email. E-commerce succeeds without investing a lot of money. It is a number one way to market Online.

> **Author's Tip:** You Don't Have to Finish your Book to Get Testimonials. Think about the people you ask. Are they busy with their business and personal life? Know that they probably won't want to read the whole book. You need to make it easy for them to "buy."

Headline: Preparing for your Testimonial Request

Write a list of ten benefits and ten features. Know that benefits sell; features describe.

Benefits are outcomes your book buyer gets after reading your book. They include more money, better relationships, better health and better life's work. Features explain what's in the book, such as pictures, stories, or how-to's.

From the benefit lists, create a few sample testimonials and keep them in your Word folder "Testimonials." Create files for book testimonials, workshop testimonials, Web site testimonials and service ones. Organizing your files and folders makes it much faster to retrieve these gems that help your sales grow.

The back cover is the author's second "Essential Hot Selling Point." People take five to ten seconds on the front cover and title. If they like it, they put in fifteen seconds on the back cover. Does your back cover have enough sizzling copy and testimonials to get readers to take out their wallets and let go of $15 to $25 of their hard-earned money in that short time?

Famous authors have learned this lesson. They put **only** testimonials on the back cover, and they include as many as they can in the front pages of their books.

Take time to create a powerful back cover. Visit your bookstore, and notice the back covers in your book's field that attract you. Copy a few sample testimonial phrases you think apply to your book. These will come in handy later, when you approach influential contacts.

Include a variety of testimonials. Put at least three testimonials on your back cover. Get one from a top professional in your field, one from a satisfied reader, one from a celebrity and one from a famous media person. While you wait for their responses, edit and re-edit the rest of your back cover copy.

One author I know wrote a book on compassionate communication. Her testimonials included an ex-convict! Not exactly the man on the street, but certainly a captive reader.

Jacqueline Marcell, author of *Elder Rage,* took eight months to get forty testimonials from celebrities. It was worth the effort, because in April 2001, she made the cover of the AARP newsletter that goes out to over 35 million readers. She had to order 10,000 more books. On top of that, she is swamped with speaking gigs. Such a problem!

Praise from others, especially recognized names, tells the reader that your book is worthy of their investment. Include testimonials in every marketing piece you do: back cover, flyers, press releases, Web pages, and your ezine or e-magazine. So you're not famous! Ask for the testimonials anyway. People in higher places want to help other authors become successful.

How to Get Those Testimonials?

1. Start early. Plan for the testimonials as you write your chapters. Mention or quote an author you used for research or a celebrity interested in your field in a few chapters. Start a list called "Mentions." These people will first become a peer editor, and then later, they may give you the gold: the testimonial!

2. Organize your "Contacts Influential." In each chapter file located in your "book folder" on your computer or in your hard copy file, the infamous manila folder, copy and paste the quote or author's book you mention with the chapter title and page number. Find out their publisher's address and write a note or send an email to ask for the testimonial.

3. Build Your List of Contacts Influential. Make friends with these people. This is what marketing is all about. Visit and comment on their Web sites, their ezines or their magazines; tell them what helped you.

Subscribe to their newsletters, and buy their books. If they are celebrities, talk to them about their favorite charity or other passion. If they are authors, tell them how much a part of their book or books helped you. Tell them you that will share their book with all of your friends and associates. If a media person, compliment them on a feature they wrote, or send them a useful article or story they may want to use. Submit useful tips. Announce your progress on your book. Like networking in professional groups, be the giver as well as the receiver. Everyone, especially people at the top, enjoys a personal note among all the business mail.

4. Network on the Internet. Submit articles that relate to your book to "Contacts Influential" Web sites. Meet them in person. Attend conferences that they speak at, such as BookExpo. Read their books, and visit their Web site often. Attend teleseminars they give. Join organizations in your field so you can network with other professionals. Start now, and keep building! When I volunteered to book speakers for a San Diego publishing group, I got to meet and make friends with Dan Poynter and John Kremmer, big names in publishing and marketing books.

5. Send each "contact influential" a short email after you have established a rapport and are halfway through writing your book. In the email, copy and paste their quoted material. Ask them if it is correct. Then mention your title and "tell-and-sell." You may want to add a bit of humor, like "I'm hoping this will warm you up a bit when I later send you a list of my book's benefits and features and a short ½ page excerpt for your opinion."

6. Author's Note: Remember your may need to contact the person 2-4 times before you get the testimonial.

7. Get peer reviews from your influential friends. Send another email asking if they will consider looking at a few pages (a partial chapter) as a favor. For this peer review, include your thirty-second "tell-and-sell," and your list of benefits and features that they can draw from to write you a specific testimonial. Tell them you will send them more if they want it. Offer a reward to those who participate: a copy of your book, perhaps.

   Author's Tip: Most people are busy and you will get more testimonials when you make it easy for them to "buy." Provide phrases that they can choose from for their convenience, or offer a choice to create their own testimonial.

8. If they request, mail by first class mail your final, professionally edited chapter. Put it in a 9 × 12-inch envelope with an SASE (return

envelope with proper postage included), so they can write right on the copy. Since you are only sending a few pages, they probably will be willing to give you corrections, ideas or quotes and to tell you what's true, what's not, what's boring and what could be omitted.

9. Prepare sample testimonials from your list of benefits that fit your book. Send a Market Survey to your friends and associates. Ask them to vote from 1-10 on each of your testimonial phrases. You may include a few of these in your final request for the gold: the testimonial from the rich and famous!

   This list will grow as you write. Add names until you have thirty. Call your folder "testimonials." Keep your lists of benefits and features in this folder.

   These will come in handy to use in all kinds of promotion later.

10. Follow up with your testimonial letter request as illustrated and directly quoted from Dan Poynter's book *Writing Nonfiction*. Since your contact has already heard from you several times, he will recognize your name and will be more willing to do you a favor by writing a short testimonial for you.

11. Collect many more testimonials each time you email or meet someone interested in your topic. Put these in your front pages of your book.

How to Write the Testimonial Letter

In *Writing Nonfiction*, Dan Poynter, guru of self-publishing, gives us an excellent example of the last letter to the "contacts influential," asking for a testimonial. Revise it for your particular needs.

Testimonial Request Letter

February 10, 2005

Walters' International
Dottie Walters
Post Office Box 1120

Dear Dottie,   **Testimonial**

I want to make you even more famous by including your prestigious name in my new book with a testimonial on page one or the back cover.

I know you are busy, and I recognize that drafting an endorsement is a creative act—requiring deep thought for most. So I have come up with a suggested line: one that ties in your background to my project. Note that it is short with a single message. Of course, you may edit this copy, change the reference to you or even start over (you are far more creative than I). You may even break my heart and blow your chance at immortality by round-filing this letter.

If you elect to take part, please make any changes on the enclosed and return it in the self-addressed, stamped envelope.

I am enclosing a mock-up of the covers along with a Table of Contents to give you an idea of the concept. Of course, I will send you a complete manuscript if you want to see it. And you will get a copy of the book as soon as it comes off the press. But please respond soon. I am (always) in a hurry.

With best regards,

PARA PUBLISHING

Dan Poynter
Publisher

DFP/ms

Using all the steps and how-to's in this special report will put you on the road to adventure, fame, and profits!

Sample Testimonial Dan Poynter Sent Me

First, I chatted with Dan at seminars, then I started sending short emails—a request, a share, a joke. Then, I asked for the testimonial. Here's what he gave me from my list of enclosed benefit and feature phrases:

"This is not a book on how to write. It is a book on how to get it written. It is full of the shortcuts, experiences and tips only an insider could know. Whether you are working on an eBook or a pBook, you will find Judy Cullins' wisdom invaluable."

—Dan Poynter,
author of *The Self Publishing Manual* and *Writing Non-Fiction*

Put your fears on the back burner, and find out how willing people are to help you get the testimonials you need to make your book a great seller.

End of report.

Bonus Report #4

The Top Ten Secrets of Successful Authors

Judy Cullins
www.bookcoaching.com

If you are not a successful author yet, incorporate the following ten secrets:

1. Treat your book as a business.

    You spend many hours creating a masterpiece to help your audience. It follows then, you need to set up a regular time schedule to market and promote it.

2. Create a flyer for each book you offer.

    Hand out your flyer at business meetings or at any public place. Ask your audience to pass the flyer along to friends and associates. Offer one free report or ezine on the flyer to get new email addresses to send promotion to later.

3. Create a line or two about your book in your signature file that goes on every email you send.

    After your name, title, and benefit statements, add something like: eBk: "Write your eBook or Other Book—Fast!" Include your addresses and phone numbers too.

4. Invest some money in book marketing.

    Contact a bookcoach and schedule a low-cost introductory session to see if you are a match and will get what you need. Many authors print too many copies or use an expensive service to get a book finished instead of putting aside an equal amount to market it.

5. Take a teleclass on how to market your book.

These low cost and low time investments can make your book the great seller it should be. Discover inexpensive ways to market via the phone and email. How convenient!

6. Don't get fooled by high-cost services.

If it's too good to be true, it isn't true. When you hire someone to do it all for you, it can cost $5000-$10,000 a publishing project, often with small results. Check out what services fit your budget, and get a realistic picture of what your results will be.

7. Delegate some of the marketing.

Like me, hire a low-cost computer assistant from your local high school. They know more than about computers and the Internet than many professionals. For under $10 an hour, you can multiply your promotion exponentially via ecommerce, your assistant does for you 2-3 times a week.

8. Set a dollar goal for your book each month.

Don't count copies sold. Count each month's book sales. Put your goal near your workstation to remind you of what you want. Don't price your book too low, so you'll appreciate an easy experience—getting what you deserve for all your work.

9. Learn more about Internet book marketing.

Think about reaching hundreds of thousands of your audience every week. When you give them what they want—free information—they will eventually buy. Many authors go the traditional path of talks, ads, or press releases. They don't always pay well for the effort.

10. Keep marketing each week.

Many clients come to me and say they are discouraged their book didn't sell well in four months. Replace doubt with patience for the process. Success takes many months, but once you get it, the Internet keeps it multiplied for you.

Knowing the secrets of successful authors can help you receive the same prestige and become a household word.

Bonus Report #5

Top Ten eBook Mistakes and How to Correct Them

Judy Cullins
www.bookcoaching.com

Did you know that you already have an eBook inside you? And, like your coach, you can earn thousands of dollars each month?

Even if you are a non-techie like me, you can write your ebook at the same time you write your print book. Or, solve your readers' problems using other articles and reports already in your files. Expand a two-page article with a story or add other how-to's.

If you want to double and triple your present book income, check out these mistakes and correct them now.

Mistake 1. You don't write a short e-Book first to test the waters

Short is in the eyes of the beholder, but let's say from 15-90 pages. Your future customers will be glad to download these pages and print only the ones they need to.

Your e-Book needs to be more concise, easy-to-read, and compelling than your print book. That means you can shorten your analogies and stories. You can use a "success format" that poses a question (a heading) your reader wants answered, then answer it. This formula gets to the point quickly, and always remember, your Online audience is busy and doesn't want a wordy style.

Mistake 2. You don't check in with a professional editor or book coach before you sell your e-Book

Yes, it's good to get feedback from peers, but you need to get a professional look at the final edition -someone who can set you straight about words and grammar that makes your writing vital and original. For instance, you need to drop your passive constructions such as "there is" or any form of "is, has, begin or start". Limit the -ly adverbs that merely tell rather than show. Your readers want a picture and want to respond with their emotions. Limit your -ing forms of the verbs. Keep your copy in present or past tense.

Mistake 3. You don't know your audience before you write your e-Book

Emerging authors make this biggest mistake. They have information, so why not write an e-Book? Instead think about the audience you will serve. More targeted works well. People who want something quick and easy that will save them time and money - another audience. The best one so far in the untapped Internet or Online audience. Mostly small business people, they are eager to buy what they need to make their life or business more enjoyable, profitable, and easy.

Right now, think of your one or two preferred audiences, and keep their profile of their needs, complaints, or problems as well as their picture by your workstation. Then you will write the book your pre-sold audience already wants!

Mistake 4. You don't automate your business

As a newbie or non-techie, at first you may resist learning how to do this. Three years ago I knew nothing about the net, and today I've published five e-Books on Internet marketing and e-Book writing and publishing. You can too, little by little.

Since each book will not bring you landslides of profit, think about limiting your small priced books. Or, bundle them so that each sale is around $20 and up.

Offer your e-Book for sale through an 800 number. One with excellent service is MRC business Support at 800-366-5596. Set up a link for people to download your book. Two companies to investigate are Clickbank.com and Paypal.com.

Delegate some of this work to your computer assistant. Contact your local high schools and technical schools where Online geniuses live. And, the cost is nominal in comparison to the results.

Mistake 5. You don't have a title that sells well

A good title is short, clear, and clever. The best title includes your book's number one benefit. Use words your audience can relate to. Even cliches are OK for book titles. Instead of "How to Market Online," offer a title like a Web site headline: "Quadruple your Monthly Book Income - Market Online."

Brainstorm a list of your possible titles with associates through a small marketing survey. Ask them to vote from 1-10 and offer their own title ideas that would make them reach into their wallets and pay $15-20 or more.

Mistake 6. You don't leverage your e-Book for higher price sales

When you look at the valuable information inside your e-Book and you realize you only make $20 a sale, you may want to investigate putting it into an e-Course. These courses sell for $79 and up. With just a little revising and tweaking, you can set your book up to be a hands-on how to course.

You can bundle several lower cost e-Books and list their singular prices. Then offer a fabulous discount to buy all three or four.

Mistake 7. You don't add bonus value to your e-Book

Whenever you put 2-4 bonus special reports at the end of your e-Book document in Portable Document Format, you make your offer so appealing, that many will buy for the bonuses alone. For an e-Book on How to Write your E-

Book or Other Book—Fast! an e-Book that sells for $24.95 at her site, the author offered these five valuable bonuses as an incentive to buy.

"The Top 10 Secrets of Successful Authors," - value $3.95, "Print on Demand (POD) Publishers—The Good, The Bad and the Ugly," - value $4.95, "How to Get Testimonials from the Rich and Famous" - value $5.95.—Dan's title value $3.95, and "The Ten eBook Mistakes and How to Correct Them," value $3.95. ($23.00 extra value).

She put a new link on her Web site "Discounts of the Month." With a limited time offer, from her e-Promotion bi-monthly offers, she got many new buyers. Everyone wants useful, original information. Everyone also wants a bargain.

Mistake 8. You put too many topics in your book

Remember, best sellers focus on one main topic. Each chapter must support that subject. When you try to give too much, your information isn't organized, short, and compelling. Instead of the end all, be all book, concentrate on one "how-to" and give plenty of details to make it useful to your reader.

Mistake 9. You don't market while you write

Most writers wish someone else would do it for them. Not in this lifetime! It's so much easier to put marketing into each chapter title, each chapter's questions you will answer, rough draft of your e-Book's back cover (sales letter), the One-Minute "Tell and Sell," and knowing your targeted audience, thesis and table of contents before you write a single chapter. Knowing these essential "Seven Hot-Selling Points" before you finish your e-Book will have you ready to promote the second you write your last word.

Mistake10. You don't brand yourself, your business, and your book

Some people join an affiliate program or set up an affiliate program for others to sell their products and sell many products. As a marketing coach, what I want for you is to think of the overview "umbrella" you can house your products under. Think about your biggest benefit you offer through your service. Think about your book title. Can you put a key word from it into each chapter title? For the book, "Passion at Any Age," the author put the word passion in each chapter title such as "Passionate Self-Care". In one client's book, "Watch Out! Your Relationships Can Be Hazardous To Your Health." the author included the key words "watch out!" in each chapter title.

The e-Book earning curve while short is important for all writers to conquer. It's easier when you contact a professional coach or take a teleclass to inform yourself. Stop making e-Book mistakes so you can earn the money you deserve.

Order Form

eBook Titles	Price	Qty.	Total
Ten Non-Techie Ways to Market Your Book Online	$34.95	_____	_____
The Fast and Cheap Way to Explode Your Targeted Web Traffic	$30.00	_____	_____
Power Writing for Web Sites that Sell	$29.95	_____	_____
San Diego Publicity Resource Book	$17.95	_____	_____
Seven Sure-Fire Ways to Publicize Your Business	$21.95	_____	_____
Quadruple Your Online Book Sales in Three Months with Free Articles	$14.95	_____	_____
How to Get Testimonials from the Rich and Famous	$5.95	_____	_____
How to Submit Articles to Web Sites: Step-by-Step	$10.95	_____	_____
Book and Writing Special Reports	$9.75	_____	_____
More Book and Writing Special Reports	$9.75	_____	_____

Total Amount

I am paying by: ☐ Cashiers Check   ☐ Credit Card   ☐ Money Order

Name on Card _____

Email _____

Website _____

Credit Card Number Expires _____

Name Phone _____

Company Phone _____

Make cashier checks payable to: Judy Cullins, Skills Unlimited

7000 Melody Lane, La Mesa, CA 91942
1/866/200-9743 (Toll-Free) – 1/619/466-0622
www.bookcoaching.com / Judy@bookcoaching.com

You may also want to subscribe to Judy's free monthly ezines: "The BookCoach Says" and "Business Tip of the Month" Dan Poynter says "its chock full of tips and resources-definitely worth your time. Go to: http://www.bookcoaching.com/opt-in.shtml

Printed in the United States
83020LV00004B/48/A